Inge Lehne — Lonnie Johnson

Vienna — The Past in the Present

A Historical Survey

D0508688

Österreichischer Bundesverlag · Wien

Cover: Schönbrunn Palace
Inset: Vienna International Centre and U-Bahn

© Österreichischer Bundesverlag Gesellschaft m.b.H., Wien 1985
Alle Rechte vorbehalten
Jede Art der Vervielfältigung, auch auszugsweise, gesetzlich verboten
Satz: Times10/11 Punkt
Gedruckt auf holzfrei Offset 120 g
Druck: Wiener Verlag, Himberg
ISBN 3-215-**05758**-1

Table of Contents

Preface 8

Introduction 10

I.   Foundations 13

         Roman Walls 14
         A New Start 15
         The Upswing 17
         The Church's Contributions 20
         The Early Heritage 22

II.   Conflicts and Consolidation 24

         New Lords: The Habsburgs 24
         Expanding the Empire and Suppressing
         Viennese Autonomy 29
         The Turkish Threat 32
         Renaissance Perspectives 33
         Internal Discord: Reformation and Counter
         Reformation 37

III.   Baroque: A Festive Society and Onlooking
         Masses 40

         Protestants, Plagues, and Turks 40
         Palaces, Pomp, and Processions 47
         Entertaining Rituals and Rituals of
         Entertainment 51
         Looking and Acting Baroque 54

IV.	Enlightenment: An Attempt at Welfare	57
	Wife, Mother, Empress, and Reformer	58
	Josephinian Innovation and Impatience	61
	Public Welfare	64
	Sobriety	67
	Artistic Impulses	71

V.	Biedermeier: A Culture of the Home	74
	Napoleon, Metternich, and the Vienna Congress	75
	Defining a Way of Life	78
	Art in and for the Home	82
	On and Off Stage	84
	The End of the Idyll	85
	The Strength of Tradition	87

VI.	The New Dimensions of the Ringstraße	89
	The Boom Years of Liberalism	89
	Petty Bourgeois Politics	92
	Working Class Misery and Social Democracy	94
	The Rise of Nationalism	96
	Starting the Ring	97
	A Ringstraße Promenade	99
	Perspectives and Parades	103

VII.	Breaking with the Past: Modern Sensibilities	105
	"To Every Age its Art; To Art its Freedom"	106
	Musical Trends	109
	New Literary Horizons	111
	The Influence of Viennese Schools	115

VIII.	The Imperial Capital Becomes a Socialist Stronghold	119
	Off to a Bad Start	121
	Old and New Cultures	125
	Red Vienna	128
	Fortress Mentalities	131
	The Violent End	134

IX.   The Nazi Interlude: Vienna, Germany 137

      The Anschluß 138
      Emigration and Reorganization 141
      Persecution of the Jews 144
      Shifts in Attitude 146
      Destruction, Resistance, and Liberation 147

X.   The Aftermath: Allied Occupation 153

      From Chaos to Order 154
      Occupation and Four Power Control 158
      Liberated but not Free 161
      Reconstruction 163
      Towards Freedom and Neutrality 164

XI.   Old Problems and New Impulses 167

      The Limitations of Innovation 168
      Traditional Structures 171
      Internationalization 173
      Traditionalisms 177

Appendix 183

      Time Line 183
      In Vienna 189
      Suggested Readings in English 194
      Selected Bibliography 195
      Index 197
      Picture Credits 200

Preface

We have tried to make this book easy to read and easy to use. At the end of the text, there is a short time line for those readers who need a quick historical orientation. This is followed by "In Vienna," a series of suggestions organized chapter by chapter dealing with things to do and see in the city. After having read a given chapter, the reader should be able to guide himself through that epoch of Viennese history by following the suggestions. There is also a brief list of selected literature and sources for readers interested in pursuing certain topics on their own.

References have been made to Austrian or European history when necessary but otherwise held to a minimum. The emphasis on history, culture, and politics shifts from chapter to chapter. This is due to the different focal points of each period. The topical emphasis of each chapter is also based on the accessibility and visibility of the past, and examples have been chosen which best illustrate the vitality and integration of traditions from different historical epochs. Assuming that they are of more immediate interest to most readers, more space has been dedicated to the 19th and 20th centuries.

Collaboration is not always easy. However, our intentions have been the same; we have tried to explain Vienna to the non-Viennese. Our backgrounds, interests, and academic trainings vary. There is a generation's age difference between us, and we have had different experiences in Vienna. Something we do have in common is that neither of us is Viennese. One of us comes from Tyrol and the other is an American from Minnesota.

Even though we contributed to and criticized each other's work, we basically divided the task of writing in two: pre-World War I Vienna (I.L.) and thereafter (L.J.). Had we each written a book, they certainly would have been different, but we hope that this one book is better than two would have been because it presents different perspectives.

We are especially indebted to Friedl and Stefan Lehne for their assistance and also would like to thank Laura Sebastian and Dr. Siegwald Ganglmair for their careful reading of the manuscript, comments, and suggestions. This book is dedicated to Friedl and Monika, our Viennese spouses and tutors.

Inge Lehne   Lonnie Johnson

Introduction

Most cities have convenient clichés which are successfully marketed for mass tourism. Venice has its gondolas, Munich its beer, Pisa its tower, London its changing of the guards, and Barcelona its bullfights. The Viennese cliché — a combination of sentimentality, waltzes, Habsburg nostalgia, choir boys, and jumping white horses — is served with *Apfelstrudel,* a double portion of whipped cream, and charm. If a foreigner does Vienna in a weekend and consumes the professionally prepared programme of obligatory sights and activities, the cliché is confirmed and reinforced. You get just what you were looking for.

Foreigners who frequently re-visit the city, stay for longer periods of time, or live and work in Vienna soon see through the cliché. This does not just apply to North and South Americans, Africans, or Asians. Germans and, in some cases, even Austrians who move to Vienna from the provinces experience the same thing. The streets of Vienna do not swing to the waltz's 3/4 time. The imperial glory of the *Ringstraße* disappears behind a haze of exhaust during rush hour. In the long run, *Wiener Schnitzel* is not as fascinating as at the beginning, and the pastries are fattening. The allegedly so charming Viennese are not familiar with the Anglo-American institution of the line, and service is not always with a smile. Changing in different social groups and settings, Viennese manners and customs appear to be a complicated ritual into which foreigners are seldom inititated. Innocent transgressions may evoke sighs, stares, or occasionally a downright rude response.

Under these circumstances the newcomer's original fascination with the city may deteriorate into a vague feeling of discomfort or even discontent. A counter-cliché develops that encompasses all of the negative aspects of Vienna, and the Viennese often contribute to this morose impression by complaining themselves. The darker side of the charming and polite Viennese personality is critical, ironic, and a bit malicious. Believing in the counter-cliché isolates some people, the Viennese as well as foreigners, and the bitter drabness of everyday Viennese reality smothers the cheery optimism of commercial exaggeration.

Enjoying Vienna involves finding some kind of middle ground between the commercial illusion of the cliché and the pessimistic blanket condemnation of the counter-cliché, an objective synthesis of the extremes. Somewhere between over-estimation and resignation, Vienna has indisputable merits. There are innumerable opportunites in the visual and performing arts. The crime rate is low. The public transportation system makes owning a car a matter of choice instead of necessity. The recreational areas in and near the city are accessible and convenient. Some Viennese make exceptions for foreigners which they would not make for their own neighbours. In addition to a high quality of life, the city has a particular aura. Vienna is indeed one of the most European cities among the continent's metropolises.

However, in comparison to other more spectacular or flamboyant European cities, Vienna is hard to get to know. Visitors are not sucked into a whirlpool of activity as they are in Rome; all of the sights to be seen are not necessarily apparent as they are in Paris. As the Viennese author Hans Weigel once wrote: "In Vienna, everything is around the corner." One of the keys to understanding and enjoying Vienna is becoming acquainted with the city's past. The Austrian novelist Heimito von Doderer described the relationship of Vienna's past to the present in the following manner: "Walking down the streets, the foliage of the past rustles around your shoes." Many outsiders to Vienna have the problem of being confronted with the foliage of the past without being able to understand or interpret it adequately. Instead of enjoying the spectacular colours, they stumble in the leaves.

The past is very present in Vienna, but it can only be seen, felt, and heard by those who develop a sense for the historical continuum of the city and its residents. This is a biography of the city designed to help foreigners develop a feeling for the personality of Vienna and the character of the Viennese. It is

11

intended for those "provisional Viennese," who have come to Vienna as a matter of choice or fate, tourists, who want to get behind the slick veneer of the commercial cliché, and historically interested arm chair travellers, who would like to visit but stay at home. Understanding the past in the present adds depth and new dimensions to experiencing Vienna.

I. Foundations

Throughout the ages, Vienna has been a border city as well as a centre of power, a market place and a battle field, a princely residence and a fortress. It was the site of sieges and diplomatic conciliation, peaceful settlements and foreign occupation. All of these phenomena have contributed to the peculiar character of the city, and understanding the development of Vienna means comprehending the extreme diversity of influences which have shaped the city as well as the mentality of its residents.

A specific geographic constellation determined the earliest foundations of Vienna. Of foremost importance is the Danube, the only major European river which runs from West to East. Its winding 2,850 km course has always connected far-flung cultures and nations; today its banks are shared by eight modern European states. Vienna is located where the Danube breaks past the last foothills of the Alps, *Kahlenberg* and *Leopoldsberg,* and turns into the shallow Vienna Basin to begin its meandering path through the Hungarian Plain.

As early as 1000 B.C., a trade route connecting the Baltic Sea with the Northern Adriatic crossed the Danube here. This naturally also increased the importance of the area for traders from Bohemia and Moravia, parts of today's Czechoslovakia, and Hungary. Archeological findings indicate that the area around Vienna has a long history of settlement. Among some of its last pre-historic inhabitants were Illyrians and Celts. However, the Vienna Basin was not only a centre of trade and peaceful communication; it was also repeatedly the scene of military confrontation. Time and again, the strategic importance of the region led to periods of warfare among rivalling ethnic groups.

Roman Walls

This story of the city begins with the Danube and the Romans. Unlike any other time in history, the Danube served as a border under the Romans. In order to protect their empire from Germanic and other hostile tribes, the Romans fortified the Southern banks of the Danube with a series of watchtowers and military camps. As a link in the chain of this defensive system, the *Limes,* they constructed *Vindobona,* a camp of admittedly second rate importance, in 100 A.D. *Vindobona* was strategically situated on high ground above one of the Danube's arms. This fact can still be appreciated by looking down toward today's *Donaukanal,* the Danube Canal, from *Ruprechtsplatz* in the Inner City. The camp was also located in between two streams, which emptied into the river at right angles, providing *Vindobona* with natural water barriers on three sides. To fortify the fourth side of the quadrangular camp, the Romans dug a broad ditch. The name of one of the busiest streets in the 1st district, *Graben,* German for moat, is a living testimony to this Roman excavation.

The Romans fortified *Vindobona* with mighty walls which were 8—10 metres high and 2—3 metres wide. Since they built all of their camps according to an established mode, it is not too difficult to trace the groundplan of the camp which covered a quarter of today's Inner City. As in other former Roman settlements, some Viennese streets still follow the course of old Roman roads. One such thoroughfare runs from *Schottentor,* down the *Herrengasse* to the Opera, and up the *Rennweg* in the 3rd district. This road linked the military camp with a civilian settlement which, as elsewhere, provided a market and places of worship.

Today it is hard to detect the heritage of Roman settlements in Vienna because the ruins have been buried deep beneath the street level by consequent centuries of development. Only exceptional circumstances, like construction on Vienna's underground transit system, the *U-Bahn,* or work on the sewage and drainage systems, give archeologists an opportunity for a subterranean glimpse of this Roman past.

In the second century, Germanic tribes broke through the Limes, but Roman legions under the command of Emperor

Marcus Aurelius regained the territories. According to one Roman historian, this emperor, successful commander, and Stoic philosopher famous for his *Meditations,* died shortly thereafter in the remote outpost of *Vindobona.*

The Viennese appear to be indebted to the Romans for introducing wine to the area. In the third century, the Romans allegedly started growing grapes to provide the soldiers with a daily ration of wine that was dispensed along with rations of bread and bacon.

A century later, the Roman Empire began to crumble. Invading Germanic tribes and then the Huns ravaged the area. *Vindobona* perished, but the enormous walls of the camp remained to provide temporary shelter for a succession of different tribes during the Great Migration and thereafter. In those days, shelter was the decisive criterion for any concentration of population, and the remains of *Vindobona* provided welcome refuge.

In the Dark Ages, very little is known about *Vindobona,* or was it *Vindomina,* a place mentioned in a history of the Goths, or *Vedunia,* a Celtic name? For years historians disagreed about what happened there. Some maintained that the Roman camp was deserted and that a new settlement was founded in the early Middle Ages. Nowadays the theory of continuous settlement is generally accepted. However, only certain corners of the camp appear to have been populated. One of the few references to the city is made in a document from 881 reporting a battle between the Franks and the Hungarians near *Wenia* which sounds remarkably like *Wien* or *Vienna.* Apart from this, no one knows much about what the settlement looked like or what happened there. Any possible description of Vienna in those times depends upon guesswork and imagination.

A New Start

By the 6th century, Bavarians had settled around Vienna, but Hungarian invasions repeatedly threatened German hegemony. This power struggle ended for a time after 955 when the German king, Otto I, decisively defeated the Hungarians in the

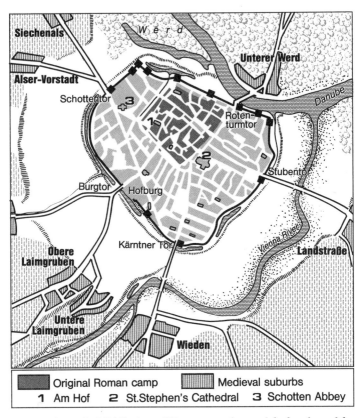

During the early Middle Ages, Vienna grew beyond the borders of the old Roman camp making new fortifications necessary

Battle of Lechfeld. This victory marks a turning point in Viennese and Austrian as well as European history. Shortly thereafter in 976, the German king entitled a member of a Franconian family, the Babenbergs, to govern the borderland in the East. Along with the Babenbergs, the name of Austria appears for the first time in a document which records their claim to *Ostarrichi,* the Eastern Realm. The Babenbergs played a crucial role in the development of Vienna for the following 270 years. In order to expand and consolidate their domains, they gradually worked their way down the Danube Valley founding residences in places like Melk, Tulln, and Klosterneuburg.

Finally, they built a castle on top of one of the hills in the Vienna Woods, *Leopoldsberg,* and from this well situated fortress they controlled the plains to the north and the east as well as the Danube.

In 1137, Vienna is referred to as a *civitas,* a city, in a contract between the diocese of Passau and the Babenbergs. The use of this particular Latin legal term indicates that Vienna was an established community with its own realm of jurisdiction and entitled to hold markets. In 1156, the Babenberg Heinrich II, who was called Jasomirgott because he allegedly used the phrase *Ja, so mir Gott helfe* (Yes, so God help me) so often, decided to make that rather insignificant little place within the old Roman walls his residence. Since Heinrich had been granted the title *Herzog* (duke), Vienna became a princely residence at this early point in its development. Heinrich set up his court *Am Hof* just inside the western wall. The name of a spacious and elegant square recalls its former prominence because *Am Hof* means "At the Court." In those days, the court was a cluster of residential building largely lacking in aristocratic grandeur. However, two Babenberg marriages to Byzantine princesses introduced the refined Eastern culture and Greek influences to the court, and it became a flourishing centre of cultural activities that attracted minstrels like Walther von der Vogelweide.

The Upswing

Vienna also began to flourish economically. Its position on the Danube made it a natural centre of trade between western regions and Hungary. The Babenbergs became rulers of Styria, south of Vienna, and this helped reactivate the old North-South trade route. They granted special privileges to merchants from Regensburg, a German city up the Danube, and Flanders, a country famous for its cloth. These western merchants were particularly interested in trade with the East. In 1221, the duke instituted the so-called "staple law" which required foreign merchants to store their goods in Vienna and put them on sale. The Viennese merchants therefore enjoyed the convenient position of middlemen who bought the goods and, in turn, resold them to the Hungarians for a handsome profit. There was, however, one local product that provided an additional basis for the flourishing trade of the Middle Ages, wine. A chronicler reports that numerous wine cellars had larger dimensions than the buildings above them, and it is still possible to explore these multi-storied caverns in many Viennese structures.

Vienna also had busy local markets where peasants and fishermen from the environs sold their goods. The names of numerous squares in the Inner City have the suffix *Markt* (market) and serve as reminders of various former centres of trade. The farmers' stands were on *Bauernmarkt,* meat was sold on *Fleischmarkt,* coal and wood were sold on *Kohlmarkt.* A visit to any one of Vienna's open air markets today brings back that unique hustling and bustling atmosphere of personal contact which is so blatantly absent in a sterile supermarket.

Vienna's increasing importance contributed to growth and prosperity, and the city spread out beyond the borders of the old Roman camp. New fortifications had to be erected to protect the growing community, and this expensive venture was apparently financed in part by a practice that nowadays would be regarded as nothing less than kidnapping. While on a crusade in the Holy Land, the Babenberg Leopold V fought side-by-side with the English King Richard the Lionhearted in the Battle of Akkon in 1189, but these comrades-in-arms parted on bad terms after a disagreement. Shortly after Leopold returned home, Richard passed through Austria on his way back to England. Aware of the imminent danger, he hid in disguise outside Vienna, but he was recognized, imprisoned in the Babenberg's Castle of Dürnstein up the Danube from Vienna, and held for ransom. The Babenbergs invested part of the enormous sum of silver the English paid to buy Richard's freedom in the new wall being built around the medieval town. This wall surrounded today's Inner City. Even though it was modernized in the 16th century, it determined the city limits of Vienna until the middle of the 19th century.

The administration of *Wiene,* as the town was called, was in the hands of a judge appointed by the Babenbergs. The City Council consisted of 24 citizens of high social and economic standing. Beneath them there was a second body of one hun-

A miniature from the Ebulo manuscript, portraying the capture of Richard the Lionhearted, in disguise, near Vienna (1197)

dred representatives elected by the average citizens from each of the town's four quarters. House ownership was a prerequisite for full citizenship and guaranteed the privilege of voting in town elections. This form of representation sheds some light on the social structure of the medieval town. The key factors in the political establishment were, on the one hand, knights, who had been entrusted with lands or granted special rights by the dukes, and, on the other, a group of powerful merchants, traders, and minters of coins.

Craftsmen were one of the most important groups in the medieval community. Organized into trade guilds, they gradually gained greater political influence. Their workshops were concentrated in certain neighbourhoods, and many of today's street names testify to their former presence. The dyers of cloth, *Färber*, were located in the *Färbergasse;* the nail and needle makers, *Nagler*, in the *Naglergasse;* the makers of arches and arrows, *Bogner*, in the *Bognergasse*, etc. The highly esteemed guilds like furriers, weapon smiths, and goldsmiths worked with the most expensive materials and for the best customers, members of the court. Day labourers and transients from many

19

walks of life occupied the largest and lowest ranks in the medieval community.

The Jews played a special role in Vienna. As non-Christians they were exempt from the Church's injunction against usury, the practice of collecting interest on loans; consequently they played a vital economic role as money lenders who generally enjoyed the duke's special protection. *Judenplatz,* Jew's Place, is right next to the former Babenberg residence *Am Hof.* The medieval Jewish ghetto was located here, and there is still a Jewish prayer-room on this square today. The Jew's special status, economic importance, foreign appearance, and religion made them unpopular with the Viennese, and they were periodically persecuted in Vienna, as elsewhere in Europe, throughout the Middle Ages.

The Church's Contributions

The dominant force in medieval Vienna was the Catholic Church, in a spiritual, moral, and, considering the number of churches in today's 1st district, also in a physical sense. Built in the 12th, rebuilt in the 13th, and expanded in the 14th century, St. Stephen's Cathedral, with its slender tower pointing like a finger into the sky, is an imposing symbol of this presence. The Viennese have always had a special relationship to their central sanctuary as well as to its tower which the Viennese still affectionately nickname *Steffl.* The pointed spire of St. Stephen's dominates the Viennese skyline on every old print and is still the highest structure in the Inner City. A building ordinance prohibits the construction of anything in the neighbourhood that could compete for attention.

The Church largely set and enforced the moral standards for the medieval community. Charity, education, health care, the lodging of pilgrims and other travelers, the documentation of births, marriages, deaths, other record keeping, and a large part of the cultural activities were in the hands of the Church. The Viennese theatrical tradition starts with the performances of passion plays in churches during the seasons of Lent and Easter.

The Church also determined the entire rhythm of medieval life. The liturgical calendar structured the year. Vacations did not exist, but abstaining from work on numerous church holidays was mandatory and provided necessary recreation. Neither clocks nor watches existed at that time, so people had to depend on the stroke of the church bell. It told them when it was time to pray, work, eat, and rest. The bell warned if the city was being attacked and alarmed residents if there was a fire. It mourned the dead and exulted to praise the Lord on days of celebration. It is easy to understand the strong ties which existed between the community and the bell.

Even though it was cast in the 17th century, the bell of St. Stephen's, *die Pummerin,* named after its low and resonant tone, symbolically represents the medieval relationship between the bell and the community. The familiar tone of the *Pummerin* has always meant a great deal to the Viennese. Destroyed at the end of World War II, the *Pummerin* was recast in Upper Austria and given to Vienna as a gift from that province in April, 1952. The Viennese were genuinely enthusiastic when the *Pummerin* returned home.

The Babenbergs supported the Church by initiating and subsidizing the construction of a great number of monasteries. One of Vienna's most important, the *Schottenstift* (Scots' Abbey) was originally built outside the walls of the city. Heinrich II Jasomirgott asked a group of Irish Benedictine monks from Regensburg in Bavaria to establish a monastery in Vienna. The confusion surrounding the Latin name for Ireland, *Scotia maior,* is responsible for mislabeling these Irish monks as Scots, *Schotten.* Even though the monks refused to learn German for 300 years, the monastery, a place of work and prayer, soon became an important cultural centre.

Secular rulers also had some ulterior motives for establishing monasteries. Generosity to the Church was generally accepted as a means of obtaining divine grace, and monasteries were symbols of secular power and prestige as well. The crypt of the *Schottenstift* also provided its generous donors with an impressive burial vault, and visitors of the abbey today can see the tombs of Heinrich, who died in 1177, his Greek wife, and daughter. The name of the square next to the abbey, the *Freyung,* also indicates that this was a sanctuary. People fleeing from persecution were "free," they could not be arrested, once they had reached the refuge of the monastic grounds. This medieval regulation was not cancelled until 1775. Many street names in the neighbourhood, *Schottentor,* a gate in the old fortifications, *Schottenbastei, Schottenring,* and *Schottengasse,* also demonstrate the presence of the abbey as well as its importance for the medieval city.

The oldest churches in Vienna are St. Ruprecht and St. Peter. The former is a very good example of early medieval architecture on a village size scale, and the later was replaced by a Baroque sanctuary in the early 18th century. Ruprecht and Peter are the patron saints of Salzburg which indicates that these churches were most likely founded by that diocese. Vienna later became part of the diocese of Passau, and St. Stephen's, commissioned by the bishop of Passau in 1137, is named after Passau's patron saint. The Babenbergs were interested in establishing a Viennese diocese in order to increase their status and prestige, but the realization of this project had to wait for centuries. The Church flourished nonetheless. By the end of the Babenberg's reign, there were over 21 churches and chapels inside of the city walls and 13 others outside in the immediate vicinity. A striking example of the church's traditional wealth and power in Vienna is the fact that it is still second largest property owner in the city today. Largest is the Municipality of Vienna itself.

The Early Heritage

The reign of the Babenberg dynasty ended in 1246 when the last male member of the line, Friedrich *der Streitbare* (the Quarrelsome) was killed in a battle with the Hungarians. He was buried near Vienna in the secluded monastery of *Heiligenkreuz* in the Vienna Woods. This monastery had been founded by one of his ancestors, Leopold III, and Vienna's *Leopoldsberg* is also named after this Babenberg who personifies his familiy's influence on the city. Leopold, which is incidentally a common Viennese name, was canonized in 1485 and made the patron saint of Austria at the end of the 17th century. The

Babenberg's dynastic colours, red-white-red, were adopted for the flag of the Austrian Republic in 1918 because they offered a strong contrast to the Habsburg's black and yellow. According to legend, one Babenberg fought so furiously in a battle during the Crusades that he was covered with blood. Afterwards, he took off his belt, discovered a red-white-red pattern on his tunic, and chose these colours for his dynastic flag.

This earliest period of Viennese history is not easily accessible to the modern observer, but traces of these early foundations are visible to an informed eye. The layout of the Inner City, certain street names, and the abundance of church buildings serve as contemporary witnesses to this important initial period of development.

II. Conflicts and Consolidation

After the death of the last Babenberg, their realm, roughly the area of today's provinces of Upper and Lower Austria and Styria, became an object of contention among ambitious princes. One of them, Ottokar of Bohemia, gained control of these territories and dreamt of creating a vast empire that would stretch from Bohemia to the Adriatic. Parts of the Austrian nobility never recognized Ottokar's controversial claim to lordship, but Ottokar won the affection of the Viennese nevertheless. He helped rebuild Vienna after two devastating fires by donating a forest to the city and initiated various building projects. It may have been his idea to move the court from *Am Hof* to a new site on the southwestern border of the city. This not only strenghtened the fortifications there but also marked the beginning of the *Hofburg,* the Court Castle, which subsequently housed the rulers of Austria. Throughout the succeeding centuries, the Hofburg grew from a small medieval quadrangle into a sprawling complex of structures built in a conglomeration of styles. Today, one wing is used for the offices of the president of the Republic of Austria.

New Lords: The Habsburgs

Ottokar ruled the Babenberg lands for thirty years before a foreigner from the West, Rudolf von Habsburg, challenged his claim. His family and name came from *Habichtsburg* (Hawk's Castle) which was in today's Swiss canton of Aargau. His election to German king had given him the right to dispose of the Babenbergs' territories as he saw fit. In 1276, a five week siege preceded Rudolf's first entry into Vienna, and the opening of the besieged city's gates mark the beginning of 640 years of Habsburg rule in Vienna. Ottokar made a final but vain attempt to regain the lost territory, but he was killed in the Battle of Marchfeld east of Vienna two years later.

Habsburg rule in Vienna did not begin very auspiciously. Even though Rudolf extended certain privileges to the Viennese in an attempt to make a good first impression, he placed his own cronies in a number of important positions. The Viennese viewed this newcomer suspiciously. Smouldering resent and economic hardship led to popular unrest that culminated in an open but unsuccessful rebellion in 1288. The Habsburgs added insult to injury by revoking privileges and curtailing citizens' rights. The following century also brought hard times upon the city. After several devastating fires, the Black Death struck Vienna in 1349 and returned a decade later.

In spite of the dark tenor of the times, the century had its high points. Another Habsburg, Rudolf IV, a young man with a grand vision, undertook everything in his power to enhance the status of Vienna and secure its position as one of the most important cities in the Holy Roman Empire. Rudolf IV was the first Habsburg to develop an ideal relationship with the city and praised it with a very personal formulation: "The city of Vienna which is the head of all our land and dominion and where we want to stay in death and life . . ."

Rudolf founded the University of Vienna in 1365. Not just an interest in education but also family rivalry was obviously one of his motives. Rudolf's father-in-law, Emperor Karl IV, had established the first Central European university in Prague in 1348. As a matter of procedure, the pope had to approve the foundation of the university, and the first classes apparently were held in St. Stephen's Cathedral. Rudolf planned to build a whole district for the university between the *Schotten* Abbey and the *Hofburg*, which would have been comparable to the Latin Quarter in Paris, but the academic centre for the following centuries developed in a neighbourhood behind St. Stephen's around today's Dr. Ignaz Seipel-Platz. Attracting students from Saxony, Bohemia, and Hungary as well as the Austrian lands, the *universitas* had an international sudent body. The seal of the University of Vienna, *Alma Mater Rudolphina*, still bears witness to Rudolf's initiative.

Rudolf also vigorously promoted the expansion of St. Stephen's. He initiated the extension of the nave of the church as

Rudolf IV, the "Founder"; allegedly the oldest individual portrait in the German speaking world (around 1365)

well as the construction of its South Tower. One motive behind this was to promote the establishment of a Viennese diocese, but this old Babenberg aspiration was something the Habsburgs were to attain only much later. Once again, family rivalry may have contributed to Rudolf's initiative; his father-in-law had St. Vitus' Cathedral built in Prague. The memory and merits of Rudolf are captured by a statue of him on the facade of St. Stephen's as well as by his Gothic burial monument inside. Visitors of the Diocesan Museum in Vienna can also see a picture of him which is allegedly the first example of portraiture in the German speaking world.

Rudolf not only expanded Vienna's cathedral, he also extended his realms. In 1363, the Habsburgs acquired Tyrol by contract and mutual agreement. Before dying at the age of 26, he had demonstrated a tremendous amount of skill and initiative, and his death left many plans and projects unfinished. Because of his prolific activity Rudolph is known as *der Stifter,* the Founder, and he certainly would have founded much more had he lived longer.

At the end of the 14th century, the Habsburg territories were divided into two (and later into three) different realms which degraded Vienna to a mere regional capital like Graz or Innsbruck. The 15th century brought hard times upon Vienna. The economic drive of the earlier Middle Ages slackened, and long-distance traders from Germany ignored the staple law causing remarkable losses for Viennese merchants. Viennese currency depreciated, and even wine trade slowed down. By the end of the century, the importance of traffic on the Danube deteriorated.

During this period, the relationship between the Viennese and their Habsburg lords grew increasingly tense; the Viennese frequently took sides against their lords in conflicts between the Habsburg family and the so-called estates: secular and ecclesiastical lords, knights, and representatives from the cities. In 1462, the Viennese went as far as declaring war on Friedrich III and besieging him in the *Hofburg,* but they inevitably ended up on the losing side. The executions of three Viennese mayors between 1412 and 1516 serve as an appalling testimony to the poor relationship Viennese subjects had to their Habsburg lords.

A detail from The Flight into Egypt by the anonymous Schotten-meister; the background shows Vienna around 1469; immediately above the Virgin's head, Minoritenkirche and the Hofburg

Friedrich III, the last Holy Roman Emperor to be crowned in Rome, finally managed to have a bishopric established for Vienna in 1468. This freed a small but important part of Austria from the ecclesiastical interference of Passau. Friedrich III is associated with a mystical puzzle consisting of the letters *A E I O U*. This stands for *Austria erit in orbe ultima,* Austria will outlive all other powers, or *Alles Erdreich ist Österreich untertan,* the entire world is Austria's subject. These letters are found on personal effects like Friedrich's diary as well as on the altars of churches and other buildings he commissioned. They also can be seen on his mighty tomb to the right of the main altar in St. Stephen's. In addition to portraying coats-of-arms and a spectrum of different animals, Friedrich's tomb, one of the grandest monuments of Gothic sculpture in Austria, is adorned with 240 statues. It took the Dutch sculptor Niclas Gerhaert van Leyden and his successors 46 years to carve this massive monument out of red and white Salzburg marble.

Two of the oldest depictions of the medieval city of Vienna date from the same time as Friedrich's tomb: panels from a Gothic altar piece portraying scenes from the life of the Virgin Mary and the Passion of Christ in the *Schotten* Abbey. One painting, the Flight into Egypt, shows Vienna from the South, and the background of the Visitation shows a side street of the *Graben.*

During Friedrich's reign, another ambitious foreigner tried to gain control of Vienna. Like Ottokar before him, the Hungarian king, Matthias Corvinus, envisioned a large Central European empire with Vienna as its heart. He drove Friedrich out of Vienna and resided in the city for five years. Legend inaccurately attributes the dominant colours on the roof of St. Stephen's, the Hungarian red, white, and green, to the presence of Corvinus. This ursurper of the Habsburg's legitimate claim to Vienna died in the city, and shortly thereafter Friedrich's son, Maximilian, festively re-entered Vienna.

Expanding the Empire and Suppressing Viennese Autonomy

Maximilian I, often called "the last of the knights," is a transitional figure to a new age, the Renaissance. The son of a Portuguese princess, he is one of the most striking figures in the long chain of rulers the Habsburg dynasty produced. Maximilian was a sportsman, renowned hunter, a bibliophile, a writer, and a patron of the arts. He also married the most eligible girl in Europe. Through his marriage to Maria of Burgundy, the Habsburgs obtained the right of inheritance to her vast domains, a territory which stretched from Eastern France up to the Flemish coast. After his wife's death, Maximilian had to fight to keep them because the French and Flemish towns were not prepared to recognize his territorial rights. Widely victorious, he became the prince of the most distinguished and refined court in Europe which reflected the gracefulness of late Gothic and the new impulses of the Renaissance. A prime

29

example of the exquisite tastes of the court, the treasures of the exclusive knightly Order of the Golden Fleece, can be seen today in the Imperial Treasury in the *Hofburg.* The famous stylized Habsburg court ceremonial also has its roots in this refined and sophisticated environment.

Vienna was located in the easternmost part of Maximilian's territories, and it lost economic and political importance as well as his attention which turned to the West and the South. After victories over the Venetians, he gained control over areas in Northern Italy. Maximilian's political and personal interests were centered on Innsbruck where he had a magnificent burial monument erected that fills more or less a whole church. Last but not least, his disinterest in Vienna may partially have been due to a bad childhood experience; the Viennese had besieged his father in the *Hofburg.*

Nevertheless, Maximilian provided Vienna with cultural and academic impulses. He founded the *Hofburgkapelle,* a court chapel, in 1498 and the *Kapellenknaben,* a boys' choir, to sing at masses and perform for the court. This choir was the forerunner of the world renowned Vienna Boys' Choir which still performs each Sunday in the Hofburg Chapel. The court's musical activities and interests paved the way for the development of Vienna's flourishing musical life in the centuries to come.

Following in his father's footsteps, Maximilian I expanded the imperial book collection which later developed into the Court Library and after 1918 was renamed the Austrian National Library. Maximilian also further promoted the university, and it developed into a flourishing academic centre which attracted professors of European standing like Konrad Celtes. The epitome of a Renaissance scholar, he had lectured in Cracow, Prague, Rome, and in German cities before coming to Vienna. Celtes, a poet laureate, held the professorial chairs for poetry and rhetoric. He contributed greatly to the court theatre, assumed the university's leading position of rector, and in this capacity initiated a series of far-reaching university reforms.

Celtes' successor, Johannes Cuspinian, was an ingenious young man of 27. Cuspinian, an adept politician and diplomat whose Renaissance burial plaque in St. Stephen's commemorates his importance, helped arrange the extraordinary Double Marriage of 1515. Maximilian's grandchildren were married to the heirs of the Bohemian and Hungarian crowns, and these marriages soon resulted in the Habsburg's inheritance of these neighbouring lands. The addition of Bohemia and Hungary to the Habsburg's domains significantly strengthened their power, increased their responsibilities, and played an important role in the future development of Vienna.

Maximilian was the most prominent of the match-making Habsburgs. He had his son married to a Spanish princess. This entitled the Habsburgs to the inheritance of Spain and Spanish territories in the New World. The Spanish marriage of Maximilian's son, combined with the acquisitions from his grandchildren's double marriage, produced a phenomenal multinational conglomeration. Even though territorial claims based on marriage often had to be reconfirmed on the battlefield, it is easy to understand the old saying *Tu felix Austria nube*: "You lucky Austria, marry."

Karl V, Maximilian's grandson, embodied the results of three generations of territorial acquisition by marriage. He ruled the traditional Habsburg realms as well as Burgundy and the vast Spanish territories. As the famous saying goes, he had an empire where "the sun never set." However, it was impossible for one man to rule these dispersed and gigantic holdings; therefore, in 1521, the territories were divided between Karl V and his brother, Ferdinand I. Ferdinand obtained the smaller part, Upper and Lower Austria, Styria, Carinthia, Carniola, now located in Northern Yugoslavia, Tyrol, and the inheritance to Bohemia and Hungary, and Karl retained the rest.

The increasing territories and power of the Habsburgs did not necessarily bring peace and prosperity to Vienna. On the contrary, the long-standing conflict between the Viennese and their Habsburg lords ended in a radical curtailment of the city's autonomy. Ferdinand arrived in Vienna shortly after assuming his territories to find the estates in rebellion. They wanted to regain rights which had been curtailed by Ferdinand's predecessor, Maximilian, but Ferdinand inconciliantly crushed the rebellion with brute force in 1522. This episode ended with the execution of the mayor and other leading figures in the revolt. A few years later, he passed a decree severely limiting citizens' rights and the city government's autonomy. Citizens were no longer allowed to independently elect the mayor and the city council, and the Habsburgs began to intervene directly in city affairs. A Habsburg appointee to the city council became the most important and powerful functionary in city government. Loyal to the Habsburgs, he enforced Viennese obedience to their lords.

This arrangement lasted for centuries. The community had been deprived of real political autonomy and subordinated to a powerful Habsburg interested in strengthening his position and control. Vienna lost its self-government to become the seat of important and princely rulers, and this consequently influenced the historical development of the community. It is also one explanation for the absence of a strong and influential upper class of proud, prosperous, and civic-minded burghers. This class, which exists in many other old European cities to date, existed in Vienna only during the Middle Ages. It took until the middle of the 19th century for the Viennese city council to regain a certain amount of municipal independence.

The Turkish Threat

In spite of the political resignation of the Viennese, the city did not slumber. There were other reasons for unrest; the Ottoman Empire posed a new threat. In the course of the preceeding two centuries, the Turks had gradually extended their influence up the Balkan peninsula, and in the early 1500's they conquered Hungary, a territory to which the Habsburgs were entitled. Vienna was considered a "bulwark of Christendom" by Christians and Moslems alike. At the end of September, 1529, the city was suddenly encircled by 300,000 Turkish troops under the leadership of Sultan Soliman II. Isolated from outside help, the Viennese were hopelessly outnumbered and trapped with their backs to the Danube.

The Turkish siege of the city lasted three weeks. The aggressors built a complicated network of trenches leading up to the city walls. Under the walls, they planted and detonated large mines in an attempt to blow a hole in the medieval fortifications. Now showing their age, the fortifications were no match for the Turkish aggressors, and the fall of the city only seemed to be a matter of time. However, in mid-October the Turks broke off the siege and left as suddenly as they had appeared. Even though they were on the verge of success, no one knows why they left so unexpectedly. Apparently they were having difficulty supplying their tremendous military force and were discouraged by the unseasonably early and snowy arrival of winter.

A few years before the Turkish siege, Vienna had been devastated by a fire, and the siege itself left the city in miserable shape. The fortifications were in shambles, and the Viennese had burned down the suburbs, which had sprung up outside of the city walls, when the Turkish troops advanced on Vienna in order to deprive the Turks of shelter. Worst of all, the Turkish army only withdrew to Hungary, and the Ottoman threat continued to cast a dark shadow over Vienna.

Renaissance Perspectives

The Turkish siege made if perfectly clear that the city's fortifications had to be renewed. Within 28 years, Italian experts and local builders constructed a star-shaped Renaissance fortress with 12 bastions around the city to replace the old damaged medieval walls. Outside of the new fortifications, they left a broad, open field called the *Glacis* where building was forbidden. The *Glacis* deprived future aggressors of cover and provided the defenders of the city with an open field of fire. The rebuilt fortifications and the *Glacis* gave Vienna a new look which was frequently depicted in etchings of the city. Some of the most famous are by Hirschvogel, Hoefnagel, and Merian.

In the 15th century, Aeneas Silvius Piccolomini, who later became pope, provided a frequently quoted description of Vienna: "The houses of the citizens are spacious and richly decorated, built solid and firm. One finds arched gates and broad courtyards everywhere. Glass windows in the houses let light stream in from all sides. The gates are mostly of iron, and on them cages with songbirds often hang. The houses have pointed

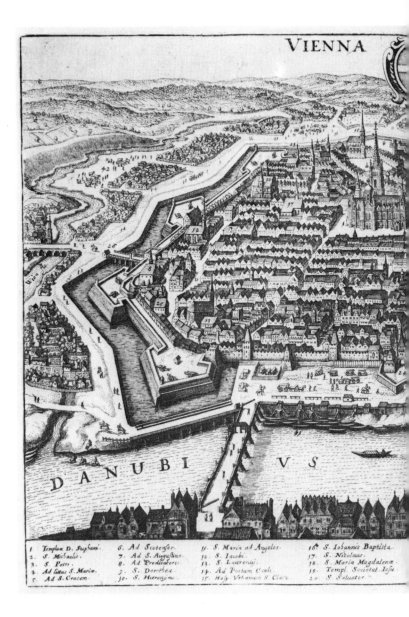

VIENNA

DANUBIVS

1. Templum D. Stephani.	6. Ad Scotenses.	11. S. Mariæ ad Angelos.	16. S. Ioannis Baptistæ.
2. S. Michaelis.	7. Ad S. Augustinæ.	12. S. Iacobi.	17. S. Nicolaus.
3. S. Petri.	8. Ad Prædicatores.	13. S. Laurentij.	18. S. Maria Magdalenæ.
4. Ad latus S. Mariæ.	9. S. Dorotheæ.	14. Ad Portam Cœli.	19. Templ Societat. Iesu.
5. Ad S. Crucem.	10. S. Hieronymi.	15. Hosp Vrbanus S. Claræ.	20. S. Saluator.

AVSTRIÆ.

FLUVIVS

26. Porta Stubensis.	31. Vniuersitas.	36. Hernals.	41. Ad Scarsos Piscator:
27. Porta Scotensis.	32. Domus Senatorum Cu.	37. Pons Altus.	42. Forum Boarium.
28. Porta Noua.	33. Arsenale.	38. Locus Sanitatis.	
29. Arx Cæsarea.	34. Domus Prætoria.	39. Domus Tinctoriana.	
30. Arx Noua.	35. Capucini.	40. Equile Cæsareum.	

*Matthäus Merian's panorama of Vienna from 1649; the late medie-
val city enclosed by its new Renaissance fortifications*

35

gables which allow a magnificent view. But it is not pretty that they make often the roofs of wood. Otherwise the houses are made of stone and decorated with paintings inside and outside".

In the 16th century, a number of contemporary reports provide more insight into the way Vienna looked and lived. Antonio de Bonfini, the court historian of the Hungarian king Corvinus, recorded the following: "The city wall is over 2,000 paces long and has thick walls to resist the biggest canons . . . The city lies like a palace in the middle of the surrounding suburbs which compete with it in beauty and size. Entering the city, you believe that you are wandering back and forth between the different buildings of a king's gigantic castle . . . The market places, the streets, and the crossroads bustle with a right pleasant and busy life . . . A tremendous amount of money is made here, but it is all spent again on food, personal appearance, and beautiful buildings."

Wolfgang Schmeltzl, a teacher at the *Schotten* Abbey's school, wrote a hymn of 1600 couplets praising Vienna:

> I praise this place above all lands.
> Here are many singers and musical hands.
> All kinds of society,
> pleasures a many.
> More instruments and music makers
> are not to be found in other places.

Humanistic interests also obviously inspired the first history of the city, *Vienna Austriae*, written by Wolfgang Lacius in 1546.

Visitors to Vienna, particularly those who have toured Italy, often wonder why the city has so few Renaissance buildings. Apart from the gate of the Salvator Church and a few smaller courtyards, the only examples of Renaissance architecture are found in the *Hofburg* complex. There is the *Stallburg,* which houses the Lipizzaner stallions of the Spanish Riding School, and the *Schweizer Tor,* the Swiss Gate, that served as an entrance to the oldest section of the *Hofburg.* This gate is named after a Swiss guard, one of the many groups of Swiss mercenaries that provided their services throughout Europe at the time, which had been retained by the Habsburgs. (The last

Swiss Guard still is in the service of the Pope in the Vatican.) Another Renaissance peculiarity can be seen at St. Stephen's. Once the decision was made not to finish the Gothic north tower of the cathedral, it was given a Renaissance cap. One of the reasons for the scarcity of Renaissance architecture in Vienna may have been the reconstruction of the city's fortifications. They devoured tremendous amounts of money that could have been spent on other projects, but the new fortifications were a question of life or death.

Internal Discord: Reformation and Counter Reformation

The Renaissance not only influenced the arts and architecture but also man's perception of himself and the world. The Protestant Reformation arose as a challenge to Catholic beliefs, institutions, and princes. The struggle between the old religion and the new dominated the entire 16th and the first half of the 17th centuries. In Vienna, a great number of people welcomed Luther's teachings, and the battle over religious questions had severe repercussions for the church in the city. Monasteries and monastic life deteriorated, and by 1550 ten of Vienna's thirteen parishes did not have priests.

Ferdinand I had been raised in Spain and introduced many Spanish customs and manners to Vienna. He attempted to bring Protestant souls back into the fold of the Catholic Church, and one of his most effective measures against Protestantism involved inviting the Jesuits to Vienna. An elite order of missionaries, the Jesuits had been founded by Ignatius of Loyola in Paris in 1534 at a time when the Church was particularly troubled. The order spearheaded the theological and political offensive against Protestantism, the Counter Reformation, and the Habsburgs carried the battle for Catholicism in Central Europe.

The Jesuits assumed influential positions throughout Vienna. Well-trained and intelligent Jesuit priests eventually became father confessors and advisors to the Habsburgs and members of the court. As missionaries, they were effective preachers. Famous as progressive educators, they also opened several schools in Vienna and were eventually entrusted with the administration of the university in 1623. Ferdinand curtailed the autonomy of the university, gave the professors the status of civil servants, and brought the institution under state control. The Jesuits administered the university for almost 150 years.

The conflict between Protestants and Catholics was bitter. The Habsburgs forbade the sale of Protestant literature, expelled Protestant preachers from the city, and introduced draconian punishments for transgressors. In 1555, the Religious Peace of Augsburg had established the principle of *cuius regio, eius religio,* literally "whose rule, his religion." This allowed secular lords to worship as they chose within the confines of their own realms and residences, but it also required subjects to practice the religion of their immediate secular lords. As a result, the majority of the Viennese are — nominally at least — Roman Catholic today. *Cuius regio, eius religio* also led to an unusual practice in Vienna. Although the Viennese Protestants were technically obligated to practice the Catholicism of their Habsburg lords, at times they left Vienna on Sundays to worship in the residences of Protestant nobility outside of the city walls.

Religious persecution and tolerance in Vienna were influenced by the ebb and the flow of the Turkish threat. This danger from the outside increased tolerance within Vienna because the feuding Christians had a common enemy. When the danger abated, internal conflicts resumed. During the reign of Maximilian II, who had obvious Protestant leanings himself, the Protestants enjoyed a significant amount of freedom in Vienna. The large majority of Viennese were Protestants at that time. For example, the medieval *Minoritenkirche* was converted into a Protestant church, and in 1576 a Protestant became mayor of Vienna. However, after Maximilian's death, the Counter Reformation resurged with greater vigor than before and lasted some 50 years. In 1585, the Habsburgs initiated a law which made Roman Catholicism the prerequisite for Viennese citizenship. Thereafter many Protestants emigrated because they refused to swear the citizen's oath on the Bible.

The leading figure in the re-Catholization of Vienna was

Melchior Khlesl, the bishop of Vienna who had converted to Catholicism after having been raised Protestant. He intitiated the so-called "monastery offensive" that fundamentally changed the medieval face of Vienna. The resurgence of Catholicism found a visible expression. Between 1603 and 1638, thirteen Catholic orders competed in an ecclesiastical building boom of monasteries and churches. This new look was imported from Italy and initially executed by Italian architects and artists. It was the style of triumphant Catholicism which turned churches into palaces, Baroque.

III. Baroque: A Festive Society and Onlooking Masses

Baroque, the period named after the style, left a particularly strong imprint on Vienna. Even though some of Vienna's most beautiful buildings are Baroque, it would be unjustified to call Vienna a Baroque city because its present appearance is basically a product of the late 19th century. The term Baroque not only refers to an artistic style; it was also an encompassing philosophy in which religion was permeated with worldliness, spirituality with sensuality, and glamour with fervour. Baroque culture reflected a way of life which was limited to the very top echelons of the social hierarchy. It flourished in an environment which was the result of a specific historical constellation.

The triumph of the Catholic Church in the Counter Reformation and the increasing power of the Habsburgs decisively influenced the development of Baroque culture. Reflected in a magnificent court life, the influence of the Habsburgs permeated Viennese society. In the early 17th century, the Habsburgs gave up the regional residences of Prague and Graz, and Vienna finally assumed a central position in the empire which it was never to lose. The city became the platform of court activities, cultural events, and an administrative and political centre of increasing importance.

Protestants, Plagues, and Turks

Vienna was also subjected to a series of trials in the 17th century. The Thirty Years War, the result of confessional conflicts, broke out in 1618. In this feud, Catholics and Protestants killed each other over theological principles as well as for practical political gains. The war endangered Vienna once in 1645 when Protestant troops from Sweden appeared north of the city.

Vienna was unprepared for an attack, and some of the wealthier Viennese fled as far as Venice. Others saw their only possible rescue in prayer. In hopes of divine intercession, the emperor organized a religious procession, and the Swedes withdrew for reasons unknown. Afterwards, a pillar-like monument dedicated to the Virgin Mary was erected *Am Hof* as a sign of gratitude.

The plague — another permanent threat — swept through Vienna in 1679 killing one third of the population of the city and its suburbs. Abraham a Sancta Clara, a famous preacher whose fire and brimstone sermons filled with puns and alliterations are not only a special genus of Baroque literature but also an inexhaustible source about the manners and customs of Baroque Vienna, described the misery in the city during the plague: "In the Lords' Street *(Herrengasse)*, Death ruled. In the Singers' Street *(Singerstraße)*, Death sang the Requiem. At the Meat Market *(Fleischmarkt)*, Death set up a butcher's bench . . . There was not a street or alley in Vienna which Death did not visit. In and around Vienna, one saw nothing other than carrying, dragging, and burying the dead."

One of a Sancta Clara's sermons also contains an episode which has been associated with a famous Viennese legend that has been immortalized by a familiar song, *Der liebe Augustin.* Augustin was a bagpipe player who had a weakness for wine. After a frivolous and drunken night, he fell asleep in the street. The victims of the plague virtually littered the streets of Vienna at that time, and Augustin was mistaken for a corpse by one of the "public maintainance crews" responsible for gathering the corpses. They picked him up, threw him onto their cart, and dumped him into one of the mass graves which had been dug for the dead. Augustin slept there all night and awoke the next morning refreshed. He crawled over the corpses and was helped out of the grave. Surviving unharmed and uninfected, he popularly personifies the typically Viennese attitudes of fatalism, stoic indifference, or even light-heartedness in the face of danger. Many people attribute his survival to the quantity of wine he had drunk.

During the plague, those who could left the city, and depopulation contributed to the plague's desolation. A monument on the *Graben* is a reminder of this catastrophe; the *Pestsäule*

*A contemporary engraving of the Siege of Vienna in 1683: fore-
ground, the fortifications and Turkish trenches surrounded by the
besieging army's tents; background, the relief armies engaging the
Turks beneath Kahlenberg and Leopoldsberg*

(Plague Column) was erected after the scourge left the city, and under the spirals of Baroque clouds and angels Emperor Leopold I can be seen kneeling in a prayer of thanks. Yet the plague had left only to return again in 1713. This time the emperor promised to build a church as a sign of gratitude as soon as the plague had passed, and the result was the Baroque landmark of Vienna, the *Karlskirche,* St. Charles Church. It was dedicated to Saint Carlo Borromeo, an Italian bishop and the patron saint of victims and survivors of the plague. The emperor's name was also *Karl* (Charles VI) so spiritual and imperial glory were combined in this masterpiece designed by Fischer von Erlach.

The border being only a day's ride from Vienna, the Turks represented another 17th century threat. After decades of peace and appeasement, it became apparent in the second half of the 17th century that Vienna, called the "Golden Apple" by the Turks, had once again become the object of the Sultan's ambitions. In July, 1683, an army of 250,000 Turks appeared south of Vienna. Within a few days, the star shaped fortifications of Vienna were enclosed by a sea of 25,000 tents. The French had signed a treaty of non-intervention with the Sultan, so Kaiser Leopold I appealed to the Pope, his own hereditary lands, the German princes, and finally Jan Sobieski, the Polish king, for help.

Although the fortifications were much better than they had been in 1529, the troops defending the city under the heroic leadership of Ernst Ruediger von Starhemberg were as hopelessly outnumbered as they had been 154 years before. There were only 11,000 soldiers supported by 5,000 armed Viennese to defend the city. The Turks and the Viennese employed the same strategies as they had in 1529. The suburbs were burned down to deprive the Turks of shelter, and the Turks built a complicated system of trenches running up to the city walls. Then they attempted to breach the fortification by planting and detonating gigantic mines.

After a 61 day siege, the Turks concentrated their attack on a bastion located near the site of today's *Burgtheater.* Just as they breached the fortifications, a relief army of 65,000 gathered on the hills north of Vienna. After mass was held in a little church on the heights, the troops, under the leadership of the Polish king Jan Sobieski and the German Prince Karl von Loth-

His reputation spread far beyond the Habsburg realms:
Prince Eugen

ringen, marched down the slopes to engage the Turks. The relief army defeated the Turks in a pitched and decisive battle that ended in a rout. The despairing Turks withdrew in disarray and left behind a tremendous amount of booty. These spoils of war happened to contain a large stockpile of coffee beans. Legend has it that these beans were given to a courageous Polish courier, Koltschitzky, who had often crossed the Turkish lines. He has been popularly regarded as the founder of the Viennese coffee house, however the first coffee house was actually established by an Armenian tradesman before the siege.

Every schoolchild in Vienna is familiar with the events surrounding the defeat of the Turks on September 12, 1683, but this date is not just of local importance. Had the Sultan taken the "Golden Apple" of Vienna, he might have had appetite for other pieces of Europa as well. The Turkish defeat at Vienna was a turning point in European history and in the expansion of the Habsburg Empire. The victorious armies pursued the Turks, and within four years Habsburg troops regained Hungary. In the following decades imperial troops conquered vast areas on the Balkan.

The ingenious military leader responsible for the expansion of the Habsburg realms was Eugenio von Savoy. The way this military genius spelled his name reveals that he was an unusual extract. He was of Italian (Eugenio) and French descent and used the German aristocratic prefix *von*. Prince Eugen had been educated at the French court, but his slight stature — he was small and had a hunchback — disqualified him for a career in the French army. In 1683, Eugen turned to the Habsburgs when they were in dire need of qualified officers, and by 1697 he was the commander-in-chief of the army. Later in his career, he also assumed top diplomatic and political functions which spanned the reigns of three Habsburg emperors.

Eugen's skills were not limited to the fields of battle and diplomacy. A personification of Baroque man, he had impeccable taste, was a patron of arts and letters, and a collector of books and maps. He is buried in St. Stephen's Cathedral, an equestrian monument on *Heldenplatz* (Heroes' Square) portrays him seated on a Lipizzaner stallion, and his books are in the National Library's most representative room, the *Prunksaal.* Two of his palaces, the *Belvedere,* which now houses museums of Austrian art, and his *Winterpalais,* the home of the Austrian Ministery of Finance, still embellish the city.

If the first Turkish siege and the consequent proximity of the Turkish threat explain the scarcity of Renaissance architecture in Vienna, then the decisive victory over the Turks after the second siege is one of the reasons for the prolificy of Baroque. The building boom was a sign of victory and confidence. Three highly gifted architects can be singled out as the

Interior of the Court Library, today's National Library, designed by
J. B. Fischer von Erlach 1722

fathers of an especially attractive and particularly Viennese type of Baroque architecture: Johann Bernhard Fischer von Erlach, who was trained in Rome, the birthplace of Baroque architecture; his son, Joseph Emanuel Fischer von Erlach; and Lukas von Hildebrandt. The architectural boom which provided these architects with a forum for their talents is in turn associated with a series of three emperors who ruled from 1658–1740: Leopold I, Joseph I, and Karl VI.

Responsible for a good part of Vienna's Baroque building, this succession of Habsburgs serve as excellent examples of the Baroque life style which was strongly influenced by Italian trends. Some members of the Habsburg familiy wrote Italian poems and others composed music in the Italian style.

Palaces, Pomp, and Processions

Ordained for his position by God to whom he was solely responsible, the Baroque emperor was the centre of political and social life. Practically all power rested in his hands. Underneath the unquestionable and supreme position of emperor, there was a complicated and highly differentiated system of ranks and privileges, the court. Participating in this hierarchy meant partaking in the power and the prestige of the emperor, and people with a modest or even insignificant role basked in their ruler's glory.

The dynastic house of the Habsburgs was identical with the state of the Habsburgs, and the court was the centre of power. Political offices were court offices, and there was no clear line between public administration and personal service. Members of the court embodied both of these functions. The decisive criterion of importance at the court was proximity to the centre of power, the emperor. The concept of proximity or closeness to power was literal as well as metaphorical. The rituals of court life regulated what, when, and how things had to be done as well as by whom. Persons of lesser importance were not even allowed in the vicinity of the emperor.

Court life was a grand stage. Ambition and competition were the driving motives of the cavalier actors; life was an exer-

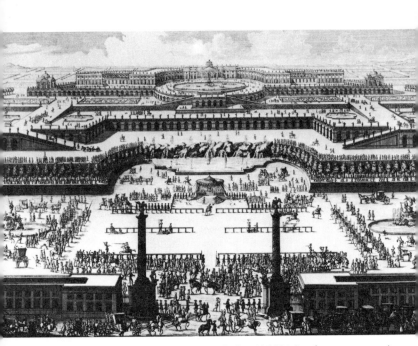

J. B. Fischer von Erlach's original plan (1690) for the summer residence of Schönbrunn; the palace assumed more modest dimensions (see cover)

cise in decorum, discipline, protocol, and intrigue. The invention of gunpowder and firearms had changed the war-like appearance of the nobility. Silk replaced outdated armour, powdered wigs took the place of helmets, and the courtier's elegance was a virtue admired as much as the knight's courage had been. During this period, the magnificent white war-horses, the Lipizzaner, were also taught to dance. Military drill provided the basis for the equestrian choreography of the Spanish Riding School.

Envy and jealousy flourished in the court atmosphere where everyone's rank and status was perfectly clear. However, Baroque man understood *Prunksucht,* literally the love of pomp or ability to impress, as a virtue, and nothing manifested a ruler's power better than monumental building. It is no coincidence that during the Baroque, the study of architecture became a key discipline in any future regent's studies. Fischer von Erlach's first plan for the Habsburg summer residence of *Schönbrunn* Palace makes it perfectly clear that the main idea was to outdo the grand dimensions of Louis the XIV's summer residence at Versailles. Palace building was a means of self-representation, and the Viennese nobility competed building in an attempt to impress the emperor as well as to outshine their peers.

In the course of the previous centuries, a cluster of aristocratic residences had developed near the *Hofburg,* but the Baroque building boom expanded this noble neighbourhood. Palaces sprung up around the *Bankgasse, Minoritenplatz, Herrengasse,* and *Josephsplatz.* The size of this aristocratic community which had been attracted to the court corresponds to the number of palaces built. At the beginning of the 18th century, approximately 25 percent of the buildings within the city fortifications were palaces.

Since the purpose of these buildings was to represent their owners, they had a number of distinctive features. The mere length of the facade was important, the longer the better. The pillared gates into the courtyards were crowned by the family's coat-of-arms which was usually under a balcony supported by muscle-bound Herculean figures, symbols of strength and power. Equal in importance was a gorgeous staircase which was not merely a means of getting up and down stairs. In the Baroque world of protocol and ceremonial, the staircase was a measure of social importance as well as an instrument of differentiation. There a decisive spectacle took place; the lord and host received his guests according to social rank and importance, step by step. Would the lord send his servant only, wait on the first or the second landing, or would he welcome his guest — probably of imperial rank — at the bottom of the staircase? The staircase was a perfect tool for the acrobatic Baroque spectacle of nearness and distance, and directions for its use were accurately laid down in the protocol of rank and privilege.

The state rooms of the palace, which were almost solely reserved for festivities, were another decisive architectural focal point. It is best to visit one of these palaces at night preferably during a ball or a reception because these social rooms should be seen in action. The mirrors multiply the festive community under the chandeliers which nowadays do not shed the mellow light of candles. (Many of the palaces are regularly rented to TV and film companies looking for authentic historical settings not to mention organizations or private individuals who seek the special atmosphere for a particularly festive occasion.) If the rooms are lit well enough, it is important to glance up at the ceiling. The skies are soft shades of pastel. Cupids and other figures — often from Greek or Roman mythology — dance across the ceiling symbolically praising the qualities of the landlord or his family. It is nice to watch the party above while being in the party below.

Organizing festivities was another means of displaying social ambitions. The aristocracy competed at entertaining with displays of fireworks, which were usually designed by architects, sleigh parties, hunts, and, last but not least, concerts which contributed to making Vienna a centre of music. Christoph W. Gluck, Joseph Haydn, and Wolfgang A. Mozart, among many others, had entertaining aristocrats as patrons, but these ingenious composers were not always treated with the respect now shown to artists. They were servants of the household who often had to wear staff uniforms.

The city palaces are often called winter palaces. After the Turkish danger had been banned, it became fashionable to spend the summer outside of the narrow confines of the fortifications. The suburbs of Vienna were fortified with the so-called *Linienwall* in 1704, which was designed to protect them from marauding tribes and bands which periodically fell into the area. This wall stood until 1890 and was located where the *Gürtel,* the busiest street in Vienna which separates the inner and outer ring of districts, is located today. Outside of the city in the wide open spaces, architects had ample opportunity to exercise their full repertoire of talents. The palaces in the city are confined compared to these summer residences which open the wings of their facades in a majestic and inviting gesture. It is no wonder that under these circumstances gardening was an ancilliary discipline of the architects. It was the extension of architectural order outside of the palace.

Old maps and an often quoted letter from a British diplomat's wife, Lady Mary Montagu, show that early 18th century Vienna was encircled with a brilliant necklace of summer residences, as a matter of fact 400 by 1740. The palaces usually overlooked geometrically planned parks and gardens which demonstrated man's ability to make the wildness of nature conform to his needs and whims. Trees and bushes were sculptured into walls and arches and mazes, and this architecturally designed landscape was peopled with all sorts of creatures in stone. The nurseries of cupids with their curls and curves are particularly enchanting, and cascades and fountains add to the playful exuberance.

Prince Eugen purchased one of the most attractive lots on the slopes outside of Vienna, and he had a magnificent summer residence built there. This gigantic project had the residual benefit of providing work for veteran soldiers who had served under him so faithfully. The roof line of the Upper Belvedere is reminiscent of Turkish war tents. From his palace southeast of Vienna, Prince Eugen had a magnificent view of the city which allowed him to look down on and at the imperial residence of the *Hofburg*. The view from this palace, which only later was named the *Belvedere,* was a favourite subject of artists. One of the finest depictions of this panorama is a painting from a series of 20 views of the city done by the Italian artist Canaletto. Exhibited in the *Kunsthistorisches Museum,* these paintings help us imagine how Vienna looked at that time.

Entertaining Rituals and Rituals of Entertainment

Other contemporary prints and paintings provide an accurate record of pageants and religious and secular processions on the *Graben* which was then the showcase of the city. There were plenty of occasions for these spectacles in the Baroque calendar: coronations, the return of victors from battle, the arrival of foreign princes or diplomats, marriages, baptisms, birthdays, patron saints' days, and especially funerals.

The celebration of death was a peculiar concern of Baroque society. Church ritual and protocol combined to honour the deceased and the majesty of death. This fascination with ritual produced a particularly Viennese burial cult which still exists in certain respects today. Some of the contemporarily most admired achievements of Baroque architects were huge constructions of decorative burial scaffolding. They were erected in churches where emperors were laid in state before burial.

For the onlooking masses, all of the people participating in these spectacles were actors, and pageants and processions provided the only form of mass entertainment. For the common man excluded from rank and privilege, there was no opportunity to directly participate in the pleasures of Baroque society. Each individual's station in the community was preordained by God and fixed at birth. The concept of equal opportunity was foreign to the Baroque world, therefore a spectacular career in the modern sense of the word was hardly a possibility. However, an enormous number of Viennese were touched by the court one way or the other.

At the end of Karl VI's reign around 1730, Vienna had a population of 40,000. Two thousand people worked for the court, and these servants and their families accounted for almost a quarter of the city's population. As the court and its offices expanded, rooms were also confiscated in the houses of normal citizens to provide direly needed space. Occasionally a modest Viennese family lived shoulder-to-shoulder with an elegant figure from the court. As a result, the common people began to imitate the mannerisms of court behaviour. The German word *höflich* and its English counterpart courteous have common origins; *Hof* means court, and *höflich* describes courtly behaviour.

The only palatial spaces open to the lowly born were the churches, but what palaces they were! The complete repertoire of Baroque splendour, illusion, and architectural wit can be found in churches. It is difficult to distinguish painted architectural detail on ceilings from real pillars, cornices, and domes; pilasters withdraw and protrude; pillars as well as side altars are multiplied; the main altar is a stage. The religious fervour of the Counter Reformation Church found its most plastic and sensual expression in the visual arts which were to provide a glorious setting for worship, sermons, music, and prayer. The theological justification for monumental building was *ad maiorem gloriam Dei,* for the greater glory of God.

Baroque was an exceedingly visible expression of piety.

However, building monumental churches and monasteries was a sign of wordly glory as well. Bishops and abbots were just as proud of their achievements as the palace building aristocray were. The beautifully designed monasteries with their ornate libraries and imperial rooms, which were reserved for visits of the most distinguished guests, have become part of the image of Austria, and there is a pun which captures this prolific period of monastic building: *Österreich − Klösterreich* (Austria, the kingdom of monasteries).

As in the past, the Church was the main carrier of education and contributed greatly to cultural activities. One of the most popular missionary vehicles of the Jesuits was the theatre. The plots of the plays were organized around the themes of virtue and sin or good and evil, and the Christian hero and the devil were the leading characters. The missionary message was lightened up with interludes of comic relief. The actors were often students who performed in Latin, but the humorous parts were always staged in the vernacular. The Jesuits also introduced unprecedented stage effects, and their productions are milestones in the development of the Viennese theatrical tradition.

The court was also another centre of Baroque dramatic activity, and a preference for musical theatre ruled there. The introduction of opera to Vienna is attributed to the Italian wife of Ferdinand III, Eleonora. Musical theatre was one form of entertainment which satisfied the complete spectrum of Baroque expectations and tastes. A production of *Pomo d'Oro,* a musical drama based on the classical tale of the Judgement of Paris, was one of the most spectacular Baroque productions. The occasion was the wedding of the emperor to a Spanish princess in 1666, and a new opera house was built especially for this event. The performance had 76 scenes, the scenery on stage was changed 23 times, the cast allegedly approached 1,000 people, the costumes were exquisite, and the stage effects excessive. Over 200 different operas were performed in Vienna during the reign of Leopold I alone. Nowadays, Vienna's opera is owned and administered by the state, and its administrators are periodically attacked for deficits or expenditures on certain productions. One tongue-in-cheek excuse is that they still work in the spirit of this lavish Baroque operatic tradition.

There was also a simple form of theatre for the common man. Actors often improvised around a loose plot, and one of the most popular characters was *Hanswurst,* a worldly joker who was bawdy, witty, and critical of those above him. Mozart's Papageno in the *Magic Flute* is a typically Viennese *Hanswurst* figure who has been transplanted into a magical setting. Even today the Viennese have a certain fascination with and weakness for theatre. This interest is not limited to attending; many individuals have either acted at some time in their lives or at least would have liked to.

Theatre is a key concept of Baroque phenomena. *Spectaculum mundi,* the idea of the world as a theatre where every man acts out the role assigned to him, permeated Baroque thought and was theologically reinforced. God had assigned everyone a station in society. Elements of drama can be found in the dynamic lines of architecture, the play of light and shadow in painting, the twist of the sculptured body, and the fascination with illusion: painted architectural elements, images multiplied by ponds or mirrors, and clever imitations of luxurious building materials like marble.

Looking and Acting Baroque

The Baroque period made a lasting impression on the Viennese, their tastes, customs, and manners. The Viennese love theatre — there are over fifty stages in the city — spectacles and the spectacular, and things with a sensual appeal. At times a preference for the theatrical "how" instead of the factual "what" can be noticed. It would be inaccurate to say that the Viennese have a particular interest in politics, but they love to watch political spectacles. Meeting places turn into stages, and an incident becomes a drama, a play.

The Viennese love of formality impresses not only foreigners but also visitors from the Austrian provinces as theatrical, and, in some cases, artificial, but rank and protocol still have a status in Vienna which is exceedingly higher than in places where real monarchies still exist. Hands are routinely kissed by members of the older generation in particular. This is a relic of the old Habsburg court ceremonial.

There is still an enormous number of titles used in Vienna. Up until 1978, 650 different titles existed in government administration, and some of them dated back to the early 17th century. A socialist government decided to rationalize and cut them back to 150, a move which many deplored. The outdated title of *Hofrat,* which literally means court advisor, is still used even though there has not been a court to advise since 1918, but this imperial title is an extremely popular and highly desired honour for the crown of a career. It would have been impossible to replace it with any republican sounding alternative. Waiters sometimes ignore guests who do not address them as *Herr Ober,* and a policeman might be annoyed if he is not addressed as *Herr Inspektor.* Some people still greet each other on the street with gracious formulations like *meine Verehrung* or *mein Kompliment,* (my respect or my compliments) and *mit vorzüglicher Hochachtung* (with exceptional high respect) is still used to end letters.

On certain occasions like marriages and funerals the spectacle, actually the ritual, of formality is completely indispensable. Guests are received according to their rank and importance or spontaneously organize themselves into the correct order in a procession. If an actor of the *Burgtheater* ensemble dies, the deceased is laid in state in the theatre's grand staircase, and thereafter the coffin is carried around the theatre in a procession. If an Austrian president dies in office, part of the burial ceremony is a procession on the *Ringstraße* in which rules of the Spanish court ceremonial are still applied to the rank and order of guests.

The ball season of *Fasching,* the Austrian version of Carneval which begins in early January and runs until Ash Wednesday, exemplifies a number of vital Baroque elements in Viennese life today. The openings of the prominent balls are complicated, festive, and carefully choreographed, and most people find them the high point of the evening. The weeks of Carneval are not only a festive season of masquerades and waltzing; they are an opportunity to display rank and order. Gentlemen embellish their tuxedoes with medals, badges, decorations, and other signs of merit. This is actually ironic because the seriousness of publicly displaying honours and rank is almost exclusively limited to a season of frivolity and masquerades.

The Viennese attitude towards social standing is also Baroque in some respects. The city has a small clique of aristocrats many of which limit their social contacts to those of similar blood and background. The entire idea of social mobility is rather foreign to most Viennese who fundamentally accept the social group into which they were born. In most higher social circles, background is more important than money. The Baroque is responsible for Viennese attitudes like a pronounced respect for people of higher social standing and a lack of social mobility.

Reactions to the Baroque heritage of Vienna are mixed. Some people dislike or even disdain the formalities and the pomp and circumstance. Others are amused to see these traditions well integrated and alive. Those with a sense for history do not see these peculiarities as hollow or amusing rituals but find them interesting.

IV. Enlightenment:
An Attempt at Welfare

A new style, a new mode of thought, and a new approach to problems followed the heyday of the Baroque. When the Enlightenment dawned on Western Europe, Baroque culture was just beginning to approach its peak in Austria. Western European in origin, the ideas of the Enlightenment penetrated Austria slowly. Having rejected the traditional authorities, the trendsetters in the West believed more in experience and reason than they did in tradition or religiosity. They questioned the very principles of Baroque world-view. Wanting to turn human affairs into an exact science, the philosophers of the Enlightenment also often disregarded the emotive and religious side of man which is so essential for an understanding of Baroque phenomena.

In Western Europe, the Enlightenment caused people to question the legitimacy of their rulers and led to the French Revolution. In Austria, however, a strong bourgeois class, the carriers and promoters of enlightenment and social change, did not exist. Enlightenment fundamentally consisted of a series of autocratic measures the Habsburgs — influenced by progressive advisors — introduced from above for the benefits of their subjects and their state. Tempered by Austria's Baroque traditions and institutions, the Enlightenment gradually caused a shift in perspective that was reflected in changes of attitude and taste. Sober economic considerations and utilitarian practices replaced opulance and flamboyant pageantry. Instead of seeing themselves exclusively as divine monarchs, the Habsburgs began to view themselves as divinely appointed public administrators. They put less and less emphasis on the spectacle of court life and found a new concern, the people.

Wife, Mother, Empress, and Reformer

Maria Theresia is a figure of transition from the opulence of the Baroque to the sobriety of the Enlightenment. As the daughter of Karl VI, she was brought up in a completely Baroque environment. When she was born in 1717, work on the *Karlskirche* had just begun, and Prince Eugene's summer palace was in its planning stages. She has justifiably been called "the daughter of an old and the mother of a new age." Due to her Baroque upbringing, Maria Theresia's approach to enlightened innovation was marked by circumspection and tempered by her own piety, loyalties to the Church, and ties of friendship to the old aristocracy. Her reforms were in most cases cautious, selective, and pragmatic.

Maria Theresia was also the only woman to rule the Habsburg realms in the long history of the dynasty. Making a number of sacrifices, her father managed to have his titles and lands transferred to a female offspring, and Maria Theresia spent the first part of her reign asserting her title and rights. After ten years of warfare and the loss of one of her most highly valued provinces, Silesia, to Friedrich II of Prussia, she consolidated her position and devoted her attention to domestic concerns.

Maria Theresia introduced a series of reforms aimed at turning the Habsburg's conglomeration of hereditary holdings into a more efficient political unit. She realized that administrative innovations could only be effective if the state could provide well-trained and educated servants to execute them. She also regarded "the education of the people as the primary task of the state." During her reign, 500 new schools were opened in her realms, 64 in Vienna alone, and she promoted the idea of mandatory primary education. She also had state schools established for educating bureaucrats and officers and created a powerful and centrally administered bureaucracy for the administration of her realms. This centralization increased the importance of Vienna, added scores of bureaucrats to the city's population, and gave civil servants a new status. The importance and presence of bureaucracy, which can still be felt in Vienna, goes back to Maria Theresia's reforms.

The empress also had the army reorganized and centralized along similar lines. The *Theresianum,* a school founded for the

Empress Maria Theresia; a portrait by M. van Meytens (1759)

training of state officials in 1746, still bears her name and now houses an elite secondary school along with the Austrian Diplomatic Academy. In Wiener Neustadt south of Vienna, the *Theresianische Militärakademie*, a cadets' school founded in 1751, is still being used by the Austrian Army to train officer candidates today.

Part of Maria Theresia's success was certainly related to the good hand she showed in picking talented and able advisors. The 19th century monument dedicated to her, located in between the twin museums on the *Ringstraße*, has her seated on the chair of state surrounded by her generals and counsellors.

Among the generals on horsebacks is Field Marshal Daun, the first recipient of the Maria Theresia Order, a medal awarded for courage and personal initiative in battle. The standing figures, just to mention a few, include Prince Kaunitz, a brilliant statesman and diplomat who arranged the first alliance with France and was a pioneer in governmental reforms; van Swieten, a Dutch doctor who laid the foundations of the Vienna Medical School, participated in the reform of the University of Vienna, and started fighting smallpox with vaccinations, a new method which was tested on several of the empress' children; and Sonnenfels, a professor of political science from the university, whose influence brought about the abolition of torture in 1766.

Maria Theresia's measures of centralization involved ruthless violations of old aristocratic rights. Her concept of morality also led to unusual practices. She established a so-called "chastity commission" to control public morality.

One can question whether Maria Theresia's enormous popularity throughout Austrian history is due to her enlightened reforms or her matriarchal and maternal manner. She moved the throne closer to the people, which, after the inaccessibility of her Baroque predecessors, made a deep and lasting impression on her subjects. For example, she announced the birth of one of her grandchildren, the first son of her second son, Leopold, informally at the *Burgtheater*. Addressing the audience in Viennese dialect, she said: *Der Poldl hat an Buam.* "Leo has a little boy." Small gestures like this endeared her to the Viennese.

Maria Theresia's marriage to Franz Stephan von Lothringen gave the dynastic line the name which the family uses to date, Habsburg-Lothringen. This was not just a typical dynastic union but a happy marriage. Maria Theresia was a loving wife and the mother of sixteen children famous for her humanity and gratitude. Once she spilled her morning coffee on the page of a file and promptly added a note apologizing for the stains. She also insisted that her beloved nanny, Countess Fuchs, be buried next to her final resting place even though the *Kaisergruft* underneath *Kapuzinerkirche* was exclusively reserved for members of the Habsburg family. Maria Theresia was able to hold the delicate balance between authority and accessibility as well as tradition and innovation. She had that peculiarly feminine instinct for knowing what things were important as well as how to manage them.

Josephinian Innovation and Impatience

Joseph II was a frustrated co-regent under his mother's supervision for 15 years before he began his ten year reign in 1780. Maria Theresia was a transitional figure; Joseph was a full-fledged representative of the Enlightenment. Consequently his vision of constructing a new state was not paired with his mother's benevolence or her sense for limitations. He was impatient, and his almost hectic radicalism actually prevented many of his innovations from producing the intended results. He wanted to do too much too fast. His sweeping plans met resistance because they conflicted with traditional interests and feelings, and his seminal ideas often fell on barren ground. Many of his reforms were withdrawn by the end of his reign or shortly thereafter simply because Joseph was in many respects ahead of his times. His innovations produced mixed responses. Thomas Jefferson said that the measures of Monsieur Habsburg showed that revolutions could be avoided. On the other hand, Friederich II of Prussia, whose enlightened innovations in many ways had been models for Joseph, accused the Habsburg reformer of "taking the second step before the first."

Joseph did not show much evidence of his mother's strict Catholicism and piety. He looked at religion from a more modern and utilitarian perspective. Shortly after his reign began, he issued the "Patent of Tolerance," a measure comparable in importance to his abolition of serfdom. Jews and Protesant denominations were given freedom to practice the religion of their choice and allowed to build their own temples and churches subject to certain architectural limitations. For example, bells, gates, and towers were not permitted. This peculiarity can be observed in several of Vienna's old non-Catholic sanctuaries.

Joseph also attempted to reduce the influence of the Church in public affairs. The official religion of the realms remained Roman Catholic and was practiced by the great

Emperor Joseph II (r.) and his brother, Leopold, Grand Duke of Tuscany; a painting by Pompeo Badoni (1769)

majority of Joseph's subjects, but the emperor insisted on the visibility of religion's usefulness. He questioned the utility of the overabundance of monasteries and convents which had either existed since the Middle Ages or been founded in the "monastery offensive" of the Counter Reformation. Parish work, education, and nursing the sick were useful religious activities, but contemplation alone served no public purpose in Joseph's eyes. He closed more than 700 monasteries and convents within his realms, 18 in Vienna alone. Streets like the *Himmelpfortgasse* or *Laurenzerberg* in Vienna's first district are reminders of the former locations of Catholic orders, and the *Dorotheum,* the state-owned auction house, is named after the former convent of St. Dorothy.

Joseph's suspension of these religious institutions was ruthless and controversial. In the process, many works of art were destroyed or lost. Church property was confiscated and sold. However, the money obtained in this way did not go into imperial pockets. It was earmarked for the so-called "Religious Fund" which was set up to pay parish priests and finance the establishment of new parishes. Joseph envisioned the parish priest as a kind of civil servant responsible for the spiritual well-being of his subjects. Therefore, he wanted the training of priests to be in the hands of the state. He also recognized the fact that these spiritual needs should be satisfied without an unnecessary waste of time or energy. An imperial decree set up the guidelines for the establishment of new parishes; no one was supposed to have to walk more than an hour to church. Joseph's interference in church affairs was extensive and occasionally assumed the character of pettiness. An imperial decree also limited the number and size of the candles which should burn on the altar during mass . . . because there was no sense in wasting wax.

Joseph's measures against the Church and its properties greatly troubled Pope Pius VI who came to Vienna in 1782 to convince Joseph of his evil ways. However, the papal advice did not stop Joseph's activities any more than Joseph's activities effected the devout Catholicism of most Viennese. Over 30,000 people collected on *Am Hof* in front of the balcony of the *Neun Chöre der Engel* Church to receive the papal blessing. Almost 200 years had to pass before there was a second papal visit to Vienna. In September, 1983, John Paul II came on a pastoral visit. Tens of thousands of people worshiped with him on *Heldenplatz* and in the *Donaupark*. He also received crowds on *Am Hof*.

Public Welfare

Joseph's reforms were by no means limited to anti-clerical measures which contributed to giving him a bad reputation among conservatives. He was exceptionally concerned about the physical well-being of his subjects and made public health one of his top priorities. Humane and utilitarian motives coincided politically; healthy subjects meant a healthy state.

Before Joseph's reign, and in 18th century Europe in general, few distinctions were made between the sick, the poor, invalids, the mentally retarded, or the insane. These people were treated fundamentally the same and isolated from the community. Joseph differentiated among these groups and had the General Hospital, *Allgemeines Krankenhaus*, built on the grounds of a former poor house. (This then modern complex has since become a protected historical monument and is still in use.) Behind the hospital, Joseph had a special building erected to isolate the mentally ill and insane. The Viennese associated the high round shape of this building with the form of a Viennese cake, the *Guglhupf*, and nicknamed it Emperor Joseph's *Guglhupf*.

The training of military surgeons was also a high priority for the emperor. He commissioned Isidore Canevale, an architect from France, to build a school for this purpose, the *Josephinum*, in 1795. The Institute for the History of Medicine is now housed behind its elegant and harmonious facade and has a singular collection of anatomical and obstetric wax models, which, on Joseph's order, were sculptured under the direction of an Italian anatomist in Florence. Nowadays it is hard to imagine how the 1192 specimens made it intact to Vienna. They were transported over the Brenner Pass by mules.

Another demonstration of Joseph's concern for the health of his subjects was the initiative he showed in opening certain

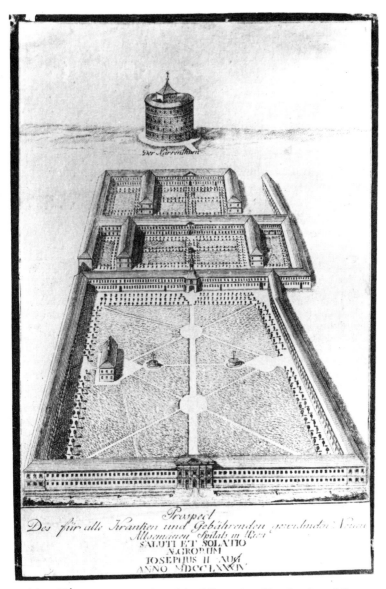

Der Narrenthurm

Prospect
Des für alle Kranken und Gebährenden gewidmeten Neuen
Allgemeinen Spitals in Wien
SALUTI ET SOLATIO
N. GRORUM
JOSEPHUS II AUG.
ANNO MDCCLXXXIV

A late 18th century engraving of the Allgemeines Krankenhaus (General Hospital) with "Joseph's Guglhupf", the insane asylum, in the background

private, imperial grounds to the public. In 1766, the *Prater*, a highly popular recreational area, was made accessible to all Viennese, and nine years later the same measure was taken with the park of the *Augarten* palace. An aristocratic woman complained to Joseph about his decision to make these places public saying: "There is no place left where we can solely enjoy society worthy of our standing." Joseph answered: "If I always wanted to be exclusively among my peers, I would have to spend the whole day in the *Kaisergruft* (Imperial Burial Vault)." These measures of Joseph are symptomatic for a trend away from aristocratic privilege towards public welfare. The inscription on the gate of the Augarten Park captures his concern and attitude: "A place of amusement dedicated to all people by their admirer."

In those days, the city proper was filthy and cramped. The Vienna Woods were not a recreational area but an impassable and dangerous wilderness. Joseph also turned the *Glacis* the open strip between the fortifications and the suburbs maintained for strategic reasons, into the prototype of an urban recreational or "pedestrian zone." He had paths made which were lined by trees and lit by lamps at night.

Tree planting was another one of Joseph's passions as well as an example of his impatience. He did not have saplings planted on the *Glacis* because it would take them too long to grow. The soldiers of his army were ordered to find, dig up, and replant more mature trees which had already reached a certain height. In Vienna to date, a city ordinance demands that every tree cut down be replaced by planting a new one, and trees are still one of the hot topics of Viennese elections. In 1973, municipal and academic authorities presented a plan which would have involved building a university institute on the site of a small park area in the 18th district. The public reaction to this project was so strong that it had to be abandoned, and the mayor resigned. Could Joseph's "environmental policies" have been responsible for the development of this passionate Viennese love of trees?

Joseph also gave public hygiene more attention. He had all of the streets inside the city walls paved with cobblestone and issued a decree demanding that the street in front of each house be wet down twice daily to keep it dust-free. Chaingangs of prisoners were used to provide a primitive form of public maintenance. The cemeteries inside the city walls were closed down, and new burial grounds were established outside of the city. Additional space and better hygiene in the city were the results.

On occasion, Joseph's enlightened maxims went too far. In 1784, he passed a new set of burial regulations which stated: "As the only purpose of the dead is to decompose, they should in future be buried unclothed, wrapped in a piece of plain cloth, and strewn with lime." Mass graves were prescribed in order not to deprive agriculture of useful ground, and all of the parishes close to the new cemetries were given rental coffins with trap doors. The dead were to be carried in them and dropped into the graves. The re-usable coffin was one way of saving wood and indicates how far Joseph's utilitarian policies and interests went. Such burial regulations demanded too much from the Viennese for whom a funeral has always been a miniature Baroque pageant. After just four months, Joseph had to retract this decree.

Sobriety

Largely due to Joseph's enlightened ideas, the atmosphere and appearance of Vienna changed considerably under his rule. He reduced ceremonial and opulence at the court and cut back the size of the imperial stables because horses were to be used for work, not parades. He disapproved of having his hand kissed, and he limited the pompous pageantry and processions associated with court birthdays, patron saint's days, and church holidays to an absolute minimum. This robbed the Viennese of one of their few and favourite forms of mass entertainment.

The "Josephinian style" of furniture and architecture was also sober and utilitarian. The period of palace building was over, and Joseph's major projects involved buildings for public use and benefit: hospitals, orphanages, barracks, etc. Simple in form and most often painted gray and white, they provide a strong contrast to the flamboyant shapes and colours of the Baroque. At this time, many palaces also passed into the hands of the state because their aristocratic owners could not afford

68

A late 18th century map of Vienna by Joseph Daniel Huber: the fortified city, the Glacis, and the expanding suburbs enclosed by the Linienwall

the upkeep of their stately homes. An architectural innovation of urban living, the apartment house, also appeared in Vienna. An early specimen that dates back to Maria Theresia still stands on the Freyung (house number 7). The Viennese called it the *Schubladkastenhaus,* the chest-of-drawers house, because they thought it resembled a piece of furniture.

The end of the 18th century was a period of expansion for Vienna. The old Baroque decree which had allowed the confiscation of private quarters for court use was retracted, and this gave the Viennese literally and figuratively more room. The suburbs outside of the city fortifications also grew rapidly. Maria Theresia had encouraged construction by suspending taxes on new buildings for twenty years, and by the end of Joseph's reign in 1790 there were three times as many houses outside of the fortifications as there were in the city itself. Streetlighting was introduced, and Joseph demanded that the streets and houses be clearly labelled and numbered. The Viennese are still spoiled in this respect because street and house markings are so clear. They often feel lost in cities abroad where street names sometimes play hide and seek.

Joseph, in particular, was interested in progress, and he recognized that a strong economy meant a solid tax base and a strong state. Vienna, traditionally a centre of trade, slowly began to develop branches of pre-industrial manufacture. Swiss clock makers settled in Vienna to start a flourishing industry. The fabrication of textiles, particularly silk, and porcelain developed in the suburbs. Vienna, a city of bureaucrats, servants, and tradesmen, now attracted manufacturers and began to develop an urban working class. The peasants, whom Joseph had freed, were attracted to the city and provided a vast reservoir of cheap labour for the manufactures. These wage earners lived under the most squalid conditions.

The enlightened Habsburgs made Vienna bigger, cleaner, greener, more important, and a better organized city. However, the political advantages of real enlightenment were not extended to the Viennese. They were still subjects, not citizens. The Habsburgs were concerned with public welfare but disinterested in public participation in political life. Enlightened monarchs saw it as their duty to think for their subjects.

Artistic Impulses

Joseph was not only interested in public projects and reorganization, he also cultivated the performing arts. Since the mid-17th century, French culture and language had been extremely fashionable in the higher ranks of Viennese society. Joseph attempted to reverse this trend and paid special attention to the German language and theatre in particular. The *Burgtheater,* Court Theatre, was given an imposing new name, *Deutsches National-Theater,* the German National Theatre, and Joseph made his predilection for organization felt once again. The theatre was financed by the court, and Joseph demanded a great amount of discipline from his actors. He passed an imperial decree forbidding that the curtain be raised for encores at the end of theatre performances, a rule which was only suspended in 1983. (The responsibility for running the court operas and theatres was assumed by the Austrian Republic in 1918. Actors at the *Burgtheater* as well as singers at the opera houses have contracts as *Beamte* or civil servants.) It is interesting to observe that the theatre flourished in the Habsburg realms inspite of the sober rationality of the Enlightenment. Not regarded merely as a form of amusement or diversion, theatre was an educational institution as well.

Maria Theresia was a very musical woman herself who had not only a pleasant voice but also was an interested patron. She appointed Christoph Willibald Gluck, who was instrumental in the development of the operatic style called "German opera," as her court composer, and the performance of a six year old child prodigy from Salzburg by the name of Wolfgang Amadeus Mozart in Schönbrunn is legendary.

Maria Theresia provided all of her children with good musical education. Joseph sang well, played the violoncello and the harpsichord, and enjoyed chamber music in his rooms after lunch. However, his musical tastes were traditional and conservative. Neither Joseph Haydn, the house composer of the noble Hungarian Esterházy family, nor Mozart enjoyed an exceptional amount of Joseph's patronage. Haydn, like so many Austrian musicians and artists after him, established his fame abroad before being recognized at home, and Mozart's Viennese career was filled with ups and downs.

The burial monument of Maria Theresia and her husband, Franz Stephan von Lothringen (background), and Joseph II's coffin (foreground) in the Kaisergruft (Imperial Burial Vault)

In 1782, Mozart's *Abduction from the Seraglio* premiered in the *Burgtheater.* The emperor did not entirely agree with the innovative role Mozart had given the orchestra. Instead of merely providing musical accompaniment, Mozart's orchestra played an essential role in the portrayal of scenes and the painting of moods. After the performance, Joseph said to the composer: "Music too beautiful for ears, dear Mozart, but a tremendous number of notes." Mozart replied: "Just as many as necessary, your Majesty." The emperor and the composer had another brief exchange after the Viennese premiere of *Don Giovanni.* "This music is lovely, divine, . . ." Joseph said, "but no food for the teeth of my Viennese." Mozart's reply was: "Then they will have to learn to chew."

Mozart maintained neither the graces of the emperor nor of the Viennese. *The Magic Flute* had its premiere in the *Theater an der Wien,* which could best be compared to an off-Broadway production today. The composer died at the age of 35, destitute and popularly neglected. Many of his biographers point out with a certain degree of pathos that his body was thrown into a common grave, but to date it remains unclear whether this was due to Mozart's poverty, an act of neglect, or the result of Joseph's revised burial codes.

Maria Theresia is one of the most popular Habsburg figures: the woman, the regent mother, and an imperial Viennese. The historical interpretation of Joseph varies. He has been called a revolutionary, an enemy of the Church, a hero of religious tolerance, a nationalist, the grandfather of Austrian liberalism, and, on very rare occasions, an unusual kind of socialist who paved the way for public welfare. Vienna owes a considerable part of its development to both of these Habsburgs. The differences in their personalities and attitudes is most clearly documented by a visit to their graves in the *Kaisergruft*. The highly ornate Rococo tomb of Maria Theresia and her husband captures them waking up, rising from the bed of death for the Resurrection. Joseph's tomb is simple and plain.

V. Biedermeier:
A Culture of the Home

Joseph, the great reformer, died in 1790, a year after the French Revolution had begun. His brother Leopold II, third in a series of enlightened rulers, assumed the throne because Joseph had no children. Leopold had ruled the Italian grand duchy of Tuscany for 25 years beforehand and is still fondly remembered there. Every now and then you meet an Italian who assures you that the administration of Tuscany is better than that of other regions due to Leopold's influence. This merely indicates what kind of potential he would have had as emperor. He combined his mother's intuition with his brother's vision, and he might have introduced a golden age of skillfully prepared, reasonable reforms had his reign not been cut short by his untimely death after a mere two years on the throne. He was succeeded by his eldest son, Franz, who ruled for 43 years under two titles: first as Franz II, Holy Roman Emperor, a title he renounced under Napoleonic pressure, and then as Franz I, Emperor of Austria, a title he had created for himself.

Franz was a tedious, reserved man whose horizons had been narrowed by the terror of the French Revolution. After all, Marie Antoinette, his father's sister, had been beheaded in 1793, and he was shocked by the possibility of similar upheavals in his own country. Franz felt equally threatened by the Industrial Revolution. No real friend of progress, he attempted to stop the construction of larger factories in Vienna by decreeing that they had to be built outside of the city. He supported the establishment of small, patriarchal businesses in the traditional Viennese field of trade and light manufacture instead. Small firms in these fields of enterprise and the absence of heavy industry are characteristic features of Vienna's economy to date. Early industrial development was underway. The first steam boat appeared on the Danube in 1818, and the first steam driven locomotive began operation outside of Vienna two decades later. However, these signs of progress were late by Western European standards. For example, in 1840, there were 1,348 km of railway tracks in England but only 144 km in Austria.

Viewing talent with suspicion and distrust, Franz found intellectuality dangerous and appreciated harmless mediocrity. An often quoted statement of his reflects this attitude. "I do not need any geniuses; all I need are good citizens." He saw himself as the father of his subjects who had to be protected from the dangers of seductive foreign influences as well as from their own follies. Franz's motto was: "Peace is the citizen's primary duty." The feelings of his subjects seem to have been mixed. He was often called the "good Kaiser Franz" and seen as a father figure particularly at the end of his reign. More mature citizens, on the other hand, disdained his paternalism.

Napoleon, Metternich, and the Vienna Congress

Wars against Napoleon took up almost 20 years of Franz's reign, and the French upstart occupied Vienna in 1805 and in 1809. Napoleon set up his quarters in *Schönbrunn* where the French eagles on the top of the obelisks in the *court d'honneur* in front of the palace can still be seen. The second occupation of Vienna was preceded by a brief siege which proved how outdated the city's fortifications were. Instead of trying to storm the walls with infantry, Napoleon's troops bombarded the city into submission. At the end of the occupation, they demonstratively blew up parts of the fortifications near the *Hofburg* to underline their uselessness. After this the fortifications lost their strategic function and assumed an almost recreational character. The paths and gangways were opened to the public and used as promenades, and the *Volksgarten*, still a lovely "park for the people," was created thereafter.

It was a small token of satisfaction for the Viennese that Napoleon suffered his first military defeat east of Vienna in the Battle of Aspern shortly after the second occupation of the city. The emperor's gifted brother, Archduke Karl, was responsible for this victory, and an equestrian monument dedicated to him stands on *Heldenplatz* as a reminder of this feat which was incidentally as transient as it was imposing. Napoleonic forces routed the Austrian army under Karl shortly thereafter at the Battle of Wagram north of Vienna.

Intending final appeasement, Franz gave the hand of his daughter Maria Louise to Napoleon in marriage. The matchmaker responsible for this marital diplomacy was Clemens Wenzel Lothar Count Metternich. Having assumed responsibility for the empire's foreign affairs in 1809, he became Franz's top aide and advisor, was elevated to the rank of prince, and was literally the leading figure in the government until 1848. Metternich, a brilliant diplomat and a sparkling star in international affairs, was often called the "Coachman of Europe." After Napoleon's final defeat, Metternich was instrumental in organizing the Congress of Vienna (1814–15) which was designed to re-arrange the map of Europe. Through it, conservatives intended to re-instate the pre-revolutionary order, suppress revolutionary ideas, and create a well-balanced network of treaties based on the Holy Alliance of Austria, Prussia, and Russia. In Metternich's eyes, this was the only guarantee for peace and harmony in Europe.

The Congress of Vienna was an unprecedented diplomatic spectacle. There were more than 700 delegates from all over Europe; two emperors, four kings, eleven princes and 90 accredited envoys brought their entire staffs, from aides and father confessors to hairdressers and parlour maids. This international community thoroughly enjoyed themselves in Vienna. Viennese aristocrats competed throwing parties, organizing balls, concerts, sleigh rides, and masquerades. After all, the Baroque tradition had provided the Viennese aristocracy with a great deal of experience and expertise in organzing festivities and celebrations. There is a theory that the image Vienna has in the world today as a city of carefree existence, dancing, and smiling originated in the fond memories of the foreign guests who were entertained so well during the Congress.

One of the delegates, Prince de Ligne, coined the phrase: *Le congrès il danse, mais il ne marche pas.* "The congress dances but it does not go forward." Much of the diplomatic work was party gossip behind the scenes. This does not speak for seriousness and the fruits of this diplomatic gossip were

Europe's diplomatic elite assembled at the Vienna Congress, 1814–15; an engraving by Jean Codefroy (1819)

questionable. In any case, the Congress did bring about more than thirty years of peace. The feelings of the Viennese during the Congress were mixed. Taxes and food prices rose but there was also money to be made, primarily by renting rooms and apartments to the guests, and there were spectacles to be watched.

Franz ruled until 1835 and was succeeded by his son, Ferdinand I, who was feeble-minded, suffered from epilepsy and was a mere puppet on the throne. This period after the Congress of Vienna and before the Revolution of 1848 has two names: *Vormärz* (Pre-March) and *Biedermeier*. The more political term of Pre-March, the revolution broke out in March 1848, connotes Metternich's system: suppression, police, secret agents, and censorship. These repressive measures were aimed at the preservation of the old order. Absolutistic practices combatted political forces which promoted liberty, equality, and fraternity as well as the nationalistic aspirations appearing on the horizons.

Intellectual development as a whole was not generally promoted but hindered. Everything had to pass the censor's desk before publication. In spite of this, there were some noticeable accomplishments. In 1815, the *Technische Hochschule,* the first higher school for the training of engineers in Central Europe, was established on *Karlsplatz,* and its buildings are still being used for that purpose. There as well as at the university more emphasis was put on teaching than on reasearch. The particular concern of the university was to educate good civil servants. An interest in historical studies was cultivated in so far as it served the glorification of the dynasty or nourished patriotism, and pioneering research was done in the field of oriental studies. As important as these achievements were, they were by no means controversial.

Pre-March is associated with frustration, persecution, and political oppression, whereas Biedermeier, the other term for this period, conjures up friendly, peaceful, cosy images. Today the term designates a style of architecture, furniture, painting, glass, china, clocks, bric-a-brac, and clothes, but it more appropriately encompasses an entire life style. Metternich's era ended in March 1848, but various aspects of Biedermeier lingered on into the 1850's as Late Biedermeier. The definite end came when the fortifications of *Alt Wien* (Old Vienna) were torn down. The *Ringstraße* marked the beginning of a new, a metropolitan period. Neither the Biedermeier way of life nor its culture were limited to Vienna alone, but the oppressive political atmosphere Franz and Metternich had created in the city contributed to the development of a retiring way of life that resulted in a very special culture of the home.

Defining a Way of Life

The term *Biedermeier* originated as a pen name and comes from the combination of the German adjective *bieder:* plain, a little naive, honest, and philistine, and the very common German surname, *Meier.* A German schoolmaster originally wrote very *bieder* types of poems which were later on satirized by two writers. They used *Biedermeier* as a pen name reflecting all of the comic attributes of that kind of poetry. The condescending attitude towards this rather narrow-minded life-style disappeared around 1900 when a new generation rediscovered not only the solid craftsmanship but also the other beauties and values of this period. The harmony of the old furniture, glass, and china were once again appreciated. People nostalgically dreamt of bygone days and of "happiness in a quiet corner." Thus the term lost its negative connotations and has since been used in a neutral manner.

What is Biedermeier? Since the days of Joseph II, the bourgeoisie had developed into a better educated, more self-assured social group. This class was located between the aristocracy and a rapidly growing population of unskilled wage earners. Biedermeier was the culture of people like lawyers, doctors, civil servants, teachers, professors, merchants, artisans, and, after the introduction of the steam engine, early industrialists. The differentiations and distinctions within this class were commonly accepted and observed. Everyone had and knew their place so to speak. The aristocrats still held the highest position on the social pyramid even though they had lost their Baroque glamour. They were also influenced by Biedermeier, appreciated a more modest appearance, and found it up-to-date to look bourgeois. Much later even the working classes began to assume some of the trappings of the Biedermeier way of life.

During the first half of the 19th century, the face of Vienna also changed. The population of the city and suburbs doubled, and most of the newcomers belonged to the pre-industrial working class. The density of the population grew, and the first real working class neighbourhoods sprung up outside of the second ring of fortifications in *Ottakring*.

Excluded from meaningful participation in public life, the bourgeoisie retreated into the seclusion of their homes, concentrated on their own privacy and their own circles, increasingly cultivated the arts, and intensified the practice of *Liebhabereien*. Literally translated, *Liebhaber* means amateur; the German term, however, has the much more positive connotation of doing something out of pure love whereas the amateur is automatically associated with a hopeless dabbler. The sheltered life within the family, friendship and harmony, and the cultivation

A Biedermeier interior

of Goodness, Truth, and Beauty were the ideals of Biedermeier men and women. The environment was the home; privacy was the ideal.

Even though the official architectural style of the period was classicism, the ambitious display of monumentalism no longer existed. Avoiding classicism's cold, white colour, Joseph Georg Kornhäusel, the outstanding architect in the Vienna area at the time, preferred *Kaisergelb* or *Schönbrunngelb,* a soft yellow, instead. The building most typical for the period was the suburban villa: a two-storied house with green shutters, a balcony supported by two columns enclosing the front door, and a gentle roof sheltering the home. The best examples of this species are concentrated in Baden, the spa 27 km south of Vienna where the court used to spend the summer vacation in those days. The town was destroyed by a fire in 1812 and rebuilt to a great extent by Kornhäusel.

For the Biedermeier home, interior space was more important than exterior display. French fashion and French trends were prevailing influences in the early 19th century throughout

Europe. The design of Biedermeier furniture was an offshoot of the elegant Empire style, but it lacks Empire's cool decoration. On the contrary, it is simple, functional, and has human dimensions. High priced on the market today, the woods used have a special grain and veneer. The interior of the Biedermeier home was decorated with a combination of practicality and love. Certain Viennese trademarks which are still associated with quality, *Bösendorfer* pianos, *Lobmeyr* glass, and *Thonet* furniture, originated as family businesses during the Biedermeier.

In 1823, when Vienna had a population of 200,000, 951 cabinet makers had their workshops in the city. During the hard years following the Napoleonic wars, woods from the country like cherry, walnut, and pear were popular. It was only after the economic recovery that luxurious mahogany was imported. Biedermeier interiors were not mass-produced. All of those lovely little desks with shining surfaces and hidden drawers reflect a high degree of artisanship, and there is a certain upright decency in all of those settees and sofas. An intimate get-together at one of those inviting round or oval tables, which were so popular at the time, is a symbol for *Gemütlichkeit.* Friends met for meals, conversation, a game of cards or chess, and, last but not least, to perform music.

During the Biedermeier period, music, which previously had been a form of entertainment limited to the court and aristocratic circles, started to be cultivated by the middle class social groups which still practice, discuss, appreciate, and cherish it today. There is a famous statement by the Viennese writer, Hans Weigel, that there is no other city in the world where dentists are such good cellists. Biedermeier Vienna, a city of some 200,000, had 65 piano factories and 2,500 chamber orchestras. In light of this, it only seems natural that the *Gesellschaft der Musikfreunde,* Society of the Friends of Music, one of the city's most valuable cultural institutions, was founded at the beginning of the Biedermeier period in 1812. The exquisite series of philharmonic concerts, which continue to be held on Saturday afternoons and Sunday mornings, was initiated in 1842. Today, a child's musical education is still a high priority for many Viennese parents, and the *Musikschule der Stadt Wien* helps train young musicians.

Art in and for the Home

An exhibition on Biedermeier culture in London in 1979 was titled "Vienna in the Age of Schubert." Franz Schubert's 20 string quartets and his 600 *Lieder* (songs) capture the Biedermeier world in a very special way. Many of these pieces were written for the gatherings of his circle of friends and first performed there. Already during his lifetime, *Schubertiade* became synonymous for these intimate musical evenings. With the exception of the waltz kings, Lanner and Strauß, Schubert was the only truly Viennese composer among the great associated with the Viennese musical tradition. The others, Gluck, Haydn, Mozart, Beethoven, Brahms, Bruckner, and Mahler, were not Viennese by birth but became Viennese by choice.

Even though Schubert's romantic songs are closely linked with Viennese Biedermeier culture, one seldom speaks of Biedermeier music. The main musical association with Biedermeier is performance and enjoyment. The music on the programme was classical and many of the minor works of the time have justifiably been forgotten today.

While we hardly speak of Biedermeier music we do speak of Biedermeier painting. It is very accessible and has a practically irresistible charm. The topics themselves are Biedermeier, man and his immediate surroundings. The paintings provide a detailed record of how people lived and looked in the Biedermeier period: their clothing, homes and gardens, children and grandparents. There are thousands of Biedermeier portraits in galleries as well as in private homes. These paintings radiate a certain feeling of self-esteem; people wanted to be captured in their Sunday's best for posterity. They look honourable, at times a bit uncomfortable, in their velvets and silks, but as soon as children come into the picture a unique idyll is created which stirs nostalgic feelings.

These "genre" paintings portray everyday life. Incidents are narrated in a realistic manner: a maiden's unhappiness about spilled milk or the tragedy of a family which has lost everything in a fire. But happiness is portrayed as well: a concert rehearsal in the open air or the rendezvous of young people in love when the roses are in bloom. The landscapes and still-lifes radiate peace and tranquility, a holiday atmosphere. Paintings were made for the home, and art was viewed as something to elevate the spirit.

Biedermeier paintings covered a broad spectrum: Amerling's portraits, Fendi's watercolours of small children, Danhauser's critical portrayals of social scenes, and Daffinger's miniatures. Rudolph von Alt documented Vienna over 70 years in oil and water colour and painted more than hundred pictures of St. Stephen's Cathedral. If you study "Old Vienna," you have to study Alt's city views. One of the most outstanding Biedermeier artists was Ferdinand Georg Waldmüller who painted pictures of the Vienna Woods with a characteristic shimmering light. This list of masters could go on and on, and there were thousands of Sunday painters who were *Liebhaber*. Water colour-painting was part of a good education, and drawing and painting were designed to teach people how to look at the world.

Franz Schubert at the piano

On and Off Stage

One of the primary Biedermeier amusements — how else could it be in Vienna — was theatre. Newly established theatres in the suburbs, the so-called *Vorstadt-Theater,* flourished and satisfied the popular demand for romance and fantasy as well as humour and cynicism. The two outstanding playwrights of the period, Ferdinand Raimund and Johann Nestroy, were actors themselves and knew the Viennese well. They set their plays in the audience's milieu and wrote in dialect. This winning combination has made their works permanent fixtures in Viennese repertoire ever since. Raimund combined the setting of everyday Biedermeier life with fantasies of fairies and magic. The wondrous solution to a hopeless situation, a modern *deus ex machina,* was executed using sophisticated and opulent theatrical techniques. Songs were intervowen in the fabric of the plays and reveal a down-to-earth and very human attitude towards life:

> People argue back and forth
> about happiness,
> They call each other stupid,
> but in the end it's just a mess.
> This is the poorest of all men
> and that one is much too rich.
> But Fate takes his carpenter's plane
> and makes them both the same.

Nestroy's puns, aphorisms, and critical comparisons, on the other hand, disclose human and social weaknesses as well as the political trends of his time. His plays epitomize the witty and often cynical Viennese sense of humour. Thornton Wilder's adaptation of Nestroy's play, *Einen Jux will er sich machen,* provided part of the story line for a famous musical, *Hello Dolly.*

There was also a tremendous amount of amateur poetry written at this time as well as an abundance of events for this *Gelegenheitsdichtung* (occasionalistic poetry): anniversaries and birthdays, patron saints' days, and public occasions. These poems are very *bieder* and sound naive and outdated today to say the least.

The poet laureate of Biedermeier literature, an author who actually transcends the period, was Franz Grillparzer. His plays reveal a deep historical insight and feeling as well as a new psychological approach. He often suffered under the censor's arbitrary decisions. There are verses in his works which ideally capture the attitude of his time:

Greatness is dangerous
and Fame a game for the vain.
It gives us empty shadows
and causes so much pain.
There is but one happiness on earth.
Just one.
A soul filled with peace and
a chest unburdened with guilt.

A true embodiment of Biedermeier ideals were the writings of Adalbert Stifter. Instrumental in institutionalizing the protection of historical monuments in Austria, he was a painter, an author, and an educator. With its ideal heroes and dedication to human values, Stifter's novel *Nachsommer* holds a special place in Austrian literature. The influence of Stifter's formulation of the "gentle law" reaches far beyond his period: "A whole life devoted to justice, simplicity, self-discipline, reasonableness, activity within its own circle, admiration of beauty, completed by a serene and calm death is what I call great . . ."

The End of the Idyll

The domestic idyll of Biedermeier culture was in many respects a reaction to Metternich's policies. However, underneath the placid surface of resignation and oppression, social tensions increased steadily. The educated wanted freedom of speech and press. Businessmen resented old fashioned restrictions that limited expansion and profit. Both groups wanted to participate in political life. The admittedly slow development of the industrial revolution had led to uneasiness on the side of the craftsmen. The workers, as elsewhere in Europe, were exploi-

The Revolution of 1848 in Vienna; a contemporary lithograph of soldiers shooting into a crowd of demonstrators

ted. The students demanded academic freedom. This general discontent was increased by economic crises in the fourties. Bad harvests and Vienna's housing shortage made the prices of food and rents jump. Bankruptcies increased unemployment. Political unrest and disturbances occured in other parts of the empire as well.

Beginning with the Paris uprising of February 1848, demands for revolutionary change swept across Europe undermining the conservative order. After different Viennese groups had respectfully submitted petitions for change to the authorities and the court, the students of the university took matters into their own hands. On March 13, 1848, they formed a procession to the *Landhaus* on *Herrengasse* to present their demands. Wanting a constitution and more liberty for the individual citizen, their goal was not the expulsion of the Habsburgs but the abolition of absolutism.

The military intervened and a commander recklessly gave the order to open fire. The revolution had its first victims. Barricades went up, the workers in the suburbs set factories on fire. To appease the angry masses the court decided to sacrifice Metternich who fled to England.

This was just the start. Different social groups had different interests and expectations, and, as a result, the revolution was an uncoordinated effort punctuated by uprisings in May, August, and October. The court fled to Innsbruck, returned to Vienna, and then fled again to Moravia. The radicalism of the masses increasingly threatened the middle class. At the end of October, imperial troops established peace and order with armed force.

Even though the revolution was unsuccessful, it had some positive effects. Forced labour of the peasants and other old feudal obligations were abolished. The revolution and an elected assembly also paved the way for the adoption of a constitution guaranteeing citizens' fundamental rights in 1867. The court was aware of the need for a change in the government. The circles closest to Ferdinand pressured him to pass the burden of rule onto his 18 year old nephew Franz Joseph. This transition took place on December 2, 1848, far away from Vienna in Olomuc, Moravia where the court had taken refuge. After the ceremony Franz Joseph formally thanked his uncle and Ferdinand replied: *Is' gern g'schehn.* "It's my pleasure."

The Strength of Tradition

The Biedermeier tradition can still be seen and felt strongly in Vienna today. Things of beauty, the past, and nature are carefully preserved and cultivated. Vandals have no great chance in the city, and the grass in the parks is treated like carpets on show. Vienna might look very different if Biedermeier care had not been practiced up until today. Cultivated craftsmanship can still be found particularly in fields where trades border the arts. More than 30 countries have their stamps engraved and printed by the *Staatsdruckerei* (Austrian State Printing House). Viennese produced chandeliers can be found in prominent places all over the world. The cakes confectioners produce are works of art, and the restoration of old furniture and books is a local speciality.

Biedermeier manners, customs, and traditions are still cultivated. The cohesiveness of family life is important and punctuated with regular get-togethers like the *Jause* of coffee and sweets on Sunday afternoons or with family celebrations. Christmas is still fundamentally a family affair celebrated in a quieter, more intimate, and less commercial manner than elsewhere. The Christmas tree was introduced to Vienna in this period, and *Silent Night,* first sung in a little village in Salzburg, is incidentally also a product of the Austrian Biedermeier.

Viennese parents feel a strong sense of responsibility for the education of their children, and according to surveys the three most frequently mentioned child rearing goals are Biedermeier in character: obedience, politeness, and thriftiness. The conservative idea of womanhood, which horrifies the women's liberation movement, the traditional wife and mother, is still a decisive role model. In spite of relative affluence, many people exercise modesty and measure. All of the Viennese enjoy good food, but their recreational habits are rather simple: a walk in the Vienna Woods and a glass of wine at a *Heurigen,* a standing-room ticket at a concert, or a trip to the *Prater.*

There are, however, two sides to the Biedermeier coin as well as some petty bourgeois elements in the Biedermeier tradition. Overdoing the virtues produces vices. The love of detail can deteriorate into a concern for trivialities. An overemphasis on privacy results in a neglect of neighbour's troubles. Biedermeier horizons often result in a lack of concern for public and international affairs. Stoic resignation degenerates into cynicism. Parental overemphasis on obedience, politeness, and thriftiness can produce neurotics instead of well-rounded young individuals. In other words, understanding Biedermeier means understanding the good and the bad in the Viennese mentality.

VI. The New Dimensions of the Ringstraße

After the spring, the fall, and the winter of the revolution, an era followed which bears the name of its emperor, the age of Franz Joseph. Spanning the terms of eighteen American presidents, his reign of 68 years encompassed a series of far reaching economic, political, and cultural transformations as well as profound changes in the ways people thought and felt. Particularly in his old age, the emperor became a symbolic figure, an element of continuity and perseverance which held together a state torn by nationalistic movements, social pressures, and innovations in the fields of science, industry, and technology. In many respects, Franz Joseph's reign marks the culmination of Vienna's development, and the outward appearance of the city today is fundamentally a product of those phenomenal decades of the *fin de siècle*. If Vienna still makes an impression of imperial grandeur, this is to a great extent due to the *Ringstraße* which was an initiative of Franz Joseph as well as an embodiment of his times.

The Boom Years of Liberalism

On the *Ringstraße* monumental public buildings and impressive private mansions of the *"Ringstraße* barons", as the business tycoons of the time were called, reflect the prosperity of the period. Next to the aristocracy of blood and a class of ennobled high-ranking civil servants and officers, a new aristocracy of achievement and money arose. As a sign of recognition, the emperor often gave successful businessmen a patent of nobility. Beer brewers and bankers were granted titles which lent their newly acquired wealth an air of legitimacy. The *Ring-*

straße barons became key factors in the social and urban development of Vienna.

In those days, a bookkeeper could open up a bank if he worked hard enough and had the necessary business acumen. Diligent hands and credit transformed workshops into factories; economic growth was furious and hectic. Between 1869 and 1873 alone, 124 new banks and 1,000 joint stock companies were founded in Austria. Not just the wealthy but also the common man indulged in speculating with stocks, and the economic bubble inevitably burst. The crash of the stock exchange in May, 1873 destroyed many large and small fortunes and ironically coincided with the opening of Vienna's World Exhibition which intended to be a celebration of prosperity and optimism.

Actually the economic recovery was soon to follow, and the large and well-off bourgeois class survived this crisis more or less intact. Cultural aspirations, a desire for elegance and refinement, soon joined the material success. The "founders" sent their sons to excellent secondary schools like the *Schottengymnasium,* the *Akademisches Gymnasium,* or the Jesuit school in Kalksburg. They studied classical and modern languages, history, and literature, and acquired impressive humanistic backgrounds. *Besitz und Bildung* (property and education) were the guiding principles of this wealthy and elite class which dominated the cultural and political life of the period.

Property was the prerequisite for participating in parliamentary, diet, and townhall politics.The right to vote was contingent upon certain tax requirements and consequently limited to 3.3% of Vienna's 700,000 residents in 1861. The 120 members of the City Council were therefore recruited from the ranks of industrialists, businessmen, doctors, lawyers, newspaper editors, and landlords. From 1861 to 1895, the city was administered by the Liberal Party whose members believed in the *laissez faire* economic principles which had so greatly contributed to their own success. During these 34 years of urban development, tremendous investments had to be made in the city's infrastructure because the densely populated "suburbs" which surrounded the city, today's districts 2—9, had been incorporated into the city 1850. This expansion made a number of important improvements necessary.

Emperor Franz Joseph in the sixty-second year of his reign, 1910

The liberals secured the city's water supply by constructing an aqueduct from the Rax Alps and Schneeberg to Vienna. After two large floods, they decided to regulate the Danube which involved draining its many arms and giving the river a new bed in the arrow straight course it has today. The huge *Zentralfriedhof* (Central Cemetry) southeast of the city was established and public transportation was extended. It consisted of a horse drawn tramway system which was privately owned.

Little attention was paid to the needs or financial limitations of the masses. Confidence in one's own ability and initiative limited the liberals' understanding for the less fortunate and deprived. Economic progress was the guiding principle of the liberals' city administration, not social concern.

Petty Bourgeois Politics

Liberalism threatened the traditional values and the economic existence of many Viennese, the petty bourgeoisie or the so-called "little man" like the shop owner, the artisan, or the small businessman in particular. Often organizing their lives around traditional Biedermeier values and Roman Catholic faith, these people managed to make a modest living. The onset of liberalism unleashed economic forces with which they could not compete. The situation of the shoemakers serves as an example; in 1852, there were only two retail shoe stores in Vienna, but by 1890, there were seventy-nine. High interest rates were common and proved to be an intolerable burden for small borrowers. Under such circumstances, a hate and fear of modern capitalism developed and frequently contained an element of anti-semitism. Jews often played a prominent role in big banks and businesses; at the same time, there was a great influx of poorer Jewish immigrants from Eastern Europe who provided additional unwanted competition. The percentage of Jews in Vienna's population rose from 1.3% in 1857 to 8% in 1910.

Anti-semitism therefore became an obvious vehicle for a populist politician. It was exploited most blatantly by Dr. Karl Lueger, a lawyer, who expressed the values, frustrations, and desires of the little man better than anybody else. He began his political career as a member of the Liberal Party, moved to the left wing, and then eventually became the leading figure in the Christian Social movement. Representing the interests of the petty bourgeoisie, Lueger promoted Christian values and a "social" political programme designed to benefit broader sections of the population. Under Lueger's leadership, the Christian Social Party developed a mass following. A reduction in tax requirements extended the right to vote to the lower middle class in 1885, and, as a result, Lueger's Christian Social Party became a major force in Viennese politics.

Lueger's popularity was immense and his closeness to the public is still proverbial. Franz Joseph thought Lueger was a demagogue and an upstart. Lueger was elected mayor four times, and each time the emperor refused to approve his appointment. Only after Lueger's fifth election in 1897, did the emperor grudgingly give the necessary approval. Lueger's 13 years as mayor were a phenomenal period in Vienna's urban development. Unlike the liberals and ahead of his times, he perceived city administration as an institution designed to serve the public. Lueger broke the monopolies private profit oriented companies had in realms of public interest like utilities and transportation. For example, to bring down the price of gas he fought a long battle with foreign owned companies which ended in turning utilities in Vienna into municipally owned and operated services. The privately owned tramways were also taken over by the city, improved, and extended. Lueger had a second aqueduct built from Styria to Vienna that greatly improved the city's water supply. He opened new hospitals, a big municipal home for the aged, over 100 schools, a public job placement office, public undertakers, communal insurance companies, and savings banks.

He was also the mayor who paved the way for today's "green Vienna," and he may be viewed as a "proto-ecologist." At a time when the dangers of pollution were hardly a common concern, he said: "Where there is room for a tree in Vienna, I wish that one be planted." Under Lueger's administration, a zone code prohibited building in the forests and meadows of the Vienna Woods. This not only limited urban sprawl but more importantly meant the preservation of the environs as a recreational area commonly called the "lungs of Vienna." This piece of legislation was the culmination of an initiative of a common citizen, Joseph Schöffel, who had started a campaign against real estate speculation and lumbering in the Vienna Woods.

Working Class Misery and Social Democracy

Lueger's period in office was a time of explosive population growth. From 1880 to 1910, the population of Vienna jumped from just over 1.1 to 2 million, and in some of his plans, Lueger envisioned a city with four million inhabitants. Lueger was an exponent of the lower middle class at a time when a rapidly growing percentage of Vienna's population consisted of blue collar workers who were excluded from the right to vote. Hundreds of thousands of immigrants were attracted to Vienna predominantly from Bohemia and Moravia. One modern testimony to this 19th century wave of immigration is the fact that there are almost as many Novaks, a common Czech name, in the Viennese telephone directory as there are in Prague's.

Not always protected by effective legislation, the living and working conditions of this class were poor. The seventy hour week was common practice. A tremendous amount of cramped residential housing was thrown up to accomodate and exploit the growing working class. Whole neighbourhoods of so-called "rent barracks" were erected outside of today's *Gürtel* where there was room for expansion and speculation. The apartments normally consisted of a room, a kitchen, and a small side room. Entire families, often seven to eight people, lived in less than 45 m^2 of space. These flats were named after the common faucet in the hall, the *Bassena,* which was the only source of water on the whole floor. A few common toilets also had to be shared by all the residents. For many of the immigrants from the country, things like running water and toilets were a great step up in the standard of living, but the overcrowded quarters were often squalid.

Rent frequently consumed 50% of the average worker's wages, and the practice of subletting beds was common. Before World War I, 17% of the Viennese were so-called *Bettgeher,* they rented a bed in some one else's flat, and 73% of the population lived in the one to two room *Bassena* apartments. Tuberculosis was so common in the city that it was known throughout Europe as the "Viennese illness."

The misery, suffering, and exploitation of the working class formed the values and ideas of another great political leader of the time. Victor Adler, regarded as the father of Austrian

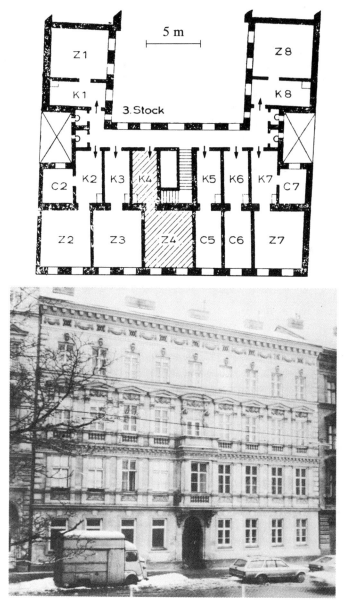

The groundplan and facade of a "rent barrack"; historicism outside, Bassena flats inside

95

Social Democracy, was the son of a wealthy Jewish family from Prague. After studying medicine, he turned down the opportunity of opening a profitable private practice and devoted himself to caring for the poor and underprivileged. Adler's medical dedication soon turned into political engagement. Undeterred by several stretches in prison, the physician was an untiring socialist activist who founded newspapers, published articles, and addressed meeting after meeting. In 1888—89, Adler realized a dream by uniting moderate socialists and radical Marxists under the auspices of the Austrian Social Democratic Workers' Party. In 1907, universal male suffrage was introduced for the elections to the *Reichsrat,* the parliament for the Austrian half of the monarchy, and the Social Democrats emerged from the election as the largest faction.

The Rise of Nationalism

The rise of nationalism also influenced the political scene in Vienna. The various minorities of the multinational empire had become increasingly restless. In 1867 Franz Joseph conceded to Hungarian demands for their own state, and the *Ausgleich* or "Compromise" created the Dual Monarchiy of Austria-Hungary. These two states were held together by their allegiance to the emperor as well as by common concerns: defense, foreign affairs, and finance. The domestic politics of each of these halves of the monarchy were handled by two different parliaments, one in Vienna and the other in Budapest, but this new constellation was no solution to the nationality problem. Although a certain degree of autonomy existed in the historical provinces of Austria, other minorities impatiently waited for more emancipation.

The rise of nationalism was also evident in certain German speaking parts of the population. German nationalist ideas had been popular ever since the Napoleonic Wars and the Revolution of 1848 in particular. Victor Adler, for example, had been a member of a Pan-Germanic fraternity as a student, but be became disillusioned with the growing racist and anti-semitic tendencies of the German nationalist movement. Radical German nationalists questioned the legitimacy of the Habsburg's multinational empire. One of their most pronounced leaders was Georg von Schönerer. The racist anti-semitism and virulent anti-Austrianism of this romantic fanatic impressed a young, poverty strickened, and frustrated art student who had failed the entrance examination to the Academy of Fine Arts, Adolf Hitler. Not only politics but also the architecture of the time influenced this young man. In *Mein Kampf,* Hitler described his first impressions of the *Ringstraße*: "From morning until late at night, I ran from one object of interest to another, but it was always the buildings which held my primary interest. For hours I could stand in front of the Opera, for hours I could gaze at the Parliament; the whole *Ringstraße* seemed to me like an enchantment out of *The Arabian Nights.*"

Starting the Ring

The Ring, as it is popularly called, is one of the great historical avenues of Europe. This proud street was the result of a proud command. An imperial decree in December 1857 began with the imperial formulation: "It is My Will . . ." This will commanded to break down the fortifications, fill the moats, link the Inner City with the newly incorporated suburbs, enhance the beauty and grandeur of the *kaiserliche und königliche Haupt- und Residenzstadt,* the Imperial and Royal Capital and Residence, and it resulted in over three decades of intensive construction.

At first there were of course many objections and protests. Aesthetic and nostalgic arguments for preserving the venerable historical appearance of the city were complemented by the admonishments of conservatives and military experts who vividly recalled the 13th of March, 1848, when workers from the suburbs attempted to support the revolution and were shut out by simply closing the old city gates. Over 165 architects from all over Europe participated in a competition to find the best design for the Ring, and they were confident that the new avenue would not only have high aesthetic standards but also meet strategic needs and concerns.

Originally a private residence, the Hoch- und Deutschmeister Palace, Parkring 8

The broad avenue of the Ring was to be spacious and monumental but also had to facilitate the quick movement of troops and make the construction of barricades in case of an uprising difficult. Military barracks were to be erected at the points where the horse shoe shaped Ring meets the Danube Canal. One of these, the *Roßauerkaserne,* has survived until today. It was built in the "Windsor style" and a technical and military accomplishment. Unfortunately insufficient attention was paid to basic human needs. When it was opened, it became evident — much to the amusement of the Viennese — that toilets had been forgotten.

The space won by razing the fortifications and the *Glacis,* the broad open field surrounding them, provided a generous amount of room for planning and construction. The authorities decided to sell lots on both sides of the avenue to citizens who were wealthy and self-assured enough to build along the Ring. Tax breaks were given to encourage buyers. In order to prevent speculation, the sales contracts stipulated that building had to start within a year and be completed within four years. These real estate sales were a huge financial success, and the profits went into a fund to finance the construction of the monumental public buildings that give the Ring its unique magnificence and splendor.

During earlier periods, the aristocracy had their palaces in the neighbourhood of the Hofburg. Now the *Ringstraße* barons built their residences along the imperial avenue. This reflects the shifts in social status. The *haute bourgeoisie* was concentrated on the most prominent and prestigious section of the Ring near the Opera, whereas members of the old aristocracy withdrew to the quieter areas of the *Parkring* near the *Stadtpark*. It is significant that the tastes of the wealthy bourgeoisie were still influenced by the model of the aristocratic lifestyle. Instead of constructing elegant townhouses as in other parts of Europe, they insisted on building palatial residences. These mansions on the Ring were in most cases "rent palaces." The proud owners had their representative apartments on the *belle etage* of the second floor, and the rest of the building, which was usually less elegant, was rented out to other parties. Even the most modest apartment in the attic had the snob appeal of a good address.

A Ringstraße Promenade

The architectural style along the Ring has been generically labelled *Ringstraßenstil.* This is a Viennese species of historicism which is not one particular style but an eclectic conglomeration of all sorts of former architectural styles. The historistic style of the *Ringstraße* was not limited to Vienna. On the contrary, it was imitated in cities all over the empire. Today travellers can still find post offices, theatres, train stations, apartment houses, etc., in Vienna's *Ringstraße* style in cities like Trieste, Cracow, Bratislava, or Sarajevo.

The Court Opera House, the first public building completed on the Ring in 1869, was inspired by the style of the Venetian Renaissance, which symbollically recalled one of the origins of opera, but it also contained Baroque and Gothic elements. Whatever the style was, the Viennese and allegedly also

The monumental buildings on the Ring

the emperor disliked the building. One of the two architects, Eduard van der Null, was so upset by the scathing criticism that he committed suicide shortly before the Opera was opened, and a few months later his colleague, August Sicard von Sicardsburg died from a heart attack. As the story goes, the emperor was so shaken by these tragic deaths that he thereafter limited his official remarks in public to a standard phrase for all occasions: *Es war sehr schön. Es hat mich sehr gefreut.* "It was very nice. I was very pleased."

The *Parlament* received a much better reception than the Opera. The Danish architect, Theophil Hansen, who had spent eight years of study in Greece, was an expert on Hellenistic architecture. The classical Greek style of the Parliament symbolically represented the democratic system of government. The neighbouring City Hall, the *Rathaus,* was designed by a

German, Friedrich von Schmidt, whose architectural speciality actually was church building. He designed seven in Vienna alone and was also responsible for the restauration of St. Stephen's at the time. The Gothic style of the *Rathaus* symbolically represented the great medieval autonomy of cities. Its main hall, which resembles the nave of a cathedral, is used for large scale representation and festivities. It can hold 1,500 waltzing couples at an annual summer ball.

The twin museums designed by Gottfried Semper and Karl von Hasenauer, the *Kunsthistorisches Museum* and the *Naturhistorisches Museum,* house the famous art gallery of the Habsburgs and a large collection on natural history. Representing flourishing arts and sciences, the architecture of these identical buildings was inspired by Renaissance forms. Like many other buildings on the Ring, a tremendous amount of space was wasted in the museums on gigantic staircases. Often covering up to a third of a building's floor space, the *Ringstraße* staircases demonstrate how important showy representation was. They also attest to the availability of real estate.

Across the Ring from the *Kunsthistorisches Museum* a new crescent shaped Neo-Baroque wing was added onto the old complex of the *Hofburg.* Just like the twin museum, this addition to the Hofburg was supposed to have an identical counterpart built across from it. The twin museums and the two wings of the *Hofburg* were to be linked by triumphal arches over the Ring. This would have created an "Imperal Forum" reminiscent of Roman greatness, but like other Austrian grand designs, this project was never executed. However, as in other cases, this incomplete project is aesthetically much more pleasing than the original plan. The vast open square was planted with grass, chestnut trees and lilac bushes. It provides a panoramic view of many of the buildings on the Ring. The two large equestrian monuments dedicated to the Austrian field marshals Prince Eugen and Archduke Karl gave this spacious opening the name of *Heldenplatz,* Heroes' Square.

Semper and Hasenauer were also entrusted with designing the Court Theatre, the *Burgtheater,* and this became one of the more controversial buildings on the Ring. The original had terrible acoustics and poorly placed seats. It had to be remodelled which led to immense overruns in cost, and the construction

The Ring nearing completion in the 1880's: Parliament, Rathaus, and the University (l. to r.)

took twice as long as planned. In the end, it was much more expensive than its larger cultural companion, the Court Opera House. In spite of these intitial difficulties, the theatre became the leading stage of the German speaking world and retained this position for a long time. *Burgtheaterdeutsch* was synonymous with perfectly articulated, accent-free German. The most attractive features of the building are two gorgeous staircases. They are decorated with murals representing the history of drama, several of which were painted by the young Gustav Klimt.

The University of Vienna moved from its old neighbourhood to a new building on the Ring next to the *Rathaus*. As a centre of learning, it was also constructed in a Renaissance style by a brilliant Viennese architect, Heinrich von Ferstel who had designed the Neo-Gothic church neighbouring the University, the *Votivkirche,* 19 years earlier. Originally planned for a student body of 3,000, the University on the Ring is now only the centre of a growing academic neighbourhood which serves 40,000 students. The parade of monumental buildings on the Ring would not be complete without mentioning Hansen's Renaissance style *Börse,* the stock exchange, or Ferstel's Museum of Applied Arts which houses, among other things, a world famous collection of oriental rugs.

Last but not least, the concert house of Vienna's Society of the Friends of Music, the *Musikverein,* should be mentioned even though it is one block off the Ring. Another Renaissance style building by Hansen, its spacious gilded concert hall is a familiar sight for the connoisseurs of globally televised concerts. It ranks among the acoustically best in the world. Next to the Opera, the *Musikverein* is Vienna's main musical centre and attraction.

Perspectives and Parades

The architecture and the monuments of the *Ringstraße* show to what extent its creators were steeped in a retrospective historical consciousness. Critics point out that building in the eclectic style of historicism was an expression of intellectual poverty or the inability to be modern, but the proponents of the Ring praise it as a major achievement in modern urban planning. Lined with four rows of trees, parks, broad sidewalks, and coffeehouses, the Ring was a festive street for festive people: for festive occasions like the leisurely Sunday strolls of the well-to-do, for seeing people and being seen, for chatty conversation and the exchange of elegant courtesies. The Ring was also planned for ceremonial parades and pageants. The silver wedding anniversary of the imperial couple, Emperor Franz Joseph and Empress Elisabeth, was celebrated in 1879. Hans Makart, the most recognized and admired painter in Vienna at the time, designed costumes, floats and banners for the parade's 14,000 participants and led the procession on a white stallion. Over

230,000 Viennese lined the Ring as spectators. Another imperial parade marked the very end of the *Ringstraße* era, the funeral procession of Emperor Franz Joseph on a cold and dark November day in 1916. Many of the mourners along the Ring may have realized that not only a monarch was being buried but also his empire.

For a long time the *Ringstraße* functioned as a show-case of the most elegant and lighthearted aspects of Viennese culture and society; eventually it became the stage, where long repressed political and social forces were released. Manifold were the flags, slogans, and ideologies of the demonstrating masses that marched down this street: Social Democrats, Christian Socials, communists, and fascists each had their day. Later came the time of the military; the German *Wehrmacht,* Russian, American, British and French occupation forces turned the street into a parade ground. Passionate political demonstrations and military troops of the past have been replaced by tens of thousands of cars today. At times the *Ringstraße* resembles a circular race course, but in every other respect more peaceful and harmonious days have returned.

It is still pleasant to walk around the *Ringstraße.* In fact, the beauty of its architecture, which for many years was looked down upon as false and pompous, is being rediscovered. It is still a festive street, one of the most striking expressions of the bright side of the Viennese spirit.

VII. Breaking with the Past: Modern Sensibilities

The "new look" of modernism replaced historicism, but the term "replaced" is not quite correct. Already gaining ground before the "old" was abandoned, the "new" style even affected the scenery of the *Ringstraße*. Otto Wagner, the great architect of Viennese art nouveau, finished the first phase of his Postal Savings Bank three years before the Ministry of Warfare, designed in the tradition of historic pomposity, was built on the opposite side of the Ring. Portraits of soldiers, along with the Habsburg's double-headed eagle with its impressive wing-spread underneath the gable, indicate the function of the building. Today the administration of the modest Austrian army does not need the entire building which now houses several Austrian ministries.

The Postal Savings Bank is a milestone of the new style. Along with Wagner's *Kirche am Steinhof,* the church of a psychiatric clinic, it has become a place of pilgrimage for art nouveau fans. Its flat facade consists of marble plates fixed by metal bolts which create an ornamental pattern. Function is turned into decoration. This idea is repeated in the main hall, where the sculptured aluminium pipes of the heating system were not concealed.

Unlike the architects of the *Ringstraße* who were oriented toward the past, Wagner committed himself to the future. Believing in the beauty of function, he adopted the motto: *artis sola domina necessitas* (use is the only master of art). Wagner took advantage of new materials like glass, concrete, aluminum and steel. He believed in a new city with new demands and finally in a new type of man. "Modern forms," he said, "must embody our own development, our democracy, our self-confidence, our idealism."

Understandably, Wagner found more rejection than appreciation in Vienna where historicism was firmly entrenched.

One of Otto Wagner's Stadtbahn stations

Most of his gigantic projects, including designs for museums, ministries, bridges, monuments, churches, and even whole districts, did not get off the drawing board. Despite this, he was involved in the two large technological projects of his time: the design of the *Stadtbahn* transit system with its bridges, tunnels and 36 stations, 20 of which remain; and the dams and quayside installations along the Danube Canal. The *Stadtbahn* stations are currently being restored just like numerous apartment buildings which have been rediscovered in a Wagner renaissance.

"To Every Age its Art; To Art its Freedom"

Under the influence of Western trends, the breach with the past took place in the most significant and drastic way in the field of fine arts. For years, Hans Makart had dominated Viennese taste in art with his pompous, historical style. His huge pannels and colourful decorations set trends and fashions which were perpetuated by lesser-known figures. The pivot of popular taste in art was the *Genossenschaft der bildenden Künstler* (Association of Fine Arts), whose exhibition centre, the *Künstlerhaus*, was on Karlsplatz next to the *Musikverein*. In 1897, the so-called 'Secessionists' broke away from the *Künstlerhaus* because they disagreed with its policies and its view of art. They wanted to familiarize the Viennese with a new type of art which should not only serve as decoration, but — and this was seen as its true purpose — should change man. A powerful drive of enthusiasm inspired these apostles to proclaim an entirely new approach to art. They organized 23 exhibitions in only seven years.

The group also built its own exhibition hall, the *Secession* building. Unlike the museums of the *Ringstraße*, which were modelled after Renaissance palaces, the *Secession* was created as a sanctuary for art. The Viennese had difficulty understanding this strange building. Interpreting the structure, they gave it a number of nick-names: the gas-furnace, Mahdi's tomb, a cross between a green house and a blast furnace. One name has survived — a friendly reference to the building's sphere of golden leaves and its close proximity to the *Naschmarkt* — *das goldene Krauthappl*, the "Golden Cabbage."

The Secession, completed 1899

The architect of the *Secession* building was one of Otto Wagner's most gifted students, Josef M. Olbrich. The inscription over the entrance-way is a programmatic motto expressing the demands of the messianic group: *Der Zeit ihre Kunst — der Kunst ihre Freiheit.* "To every age its art; to art its freedom." The man who guided the Secessionists was an artist of high stature, Gustav Klimt. As a young painter on the *Ringstraße*, Klimt had followed traditional practices; however, growing out of these, he adopted a new style which the authorities responsible for public commissions found hard to understand. In spite of this, within a few years his reputation, particularly as a portrait artist, spread and became firmly established. Among the ladies of the rich bourgeoise, it became a status symbol to be portayed by Klimt.

The members of the Secession — painters, sculptors, architects and designers — believed that their art would create a new and better world. New art would bring about a new feeling of life, pure and true, free from pretence and hypocrisy. The group expressed its beliefs not only through its exhibition hall but also with its own periodical, the *Ver Sacrum* (Sacred Spring). First published in 1898, the year the *Secession* was opened, every edition of *Ver Sacrum* represented and proclaimed the beliefs of the young artists and their literary counterparts.

This almost religious faith in the importance of art was also expressed in the programme of the *Wiener Werkstätte,* the Vienna Workshops. Founded in 1903 by Joseph Hoffman, another highly gifted student of Otto Wagner, Kolo Moser and Fritz Waerndorfer, who offered a financial basis, the *Wiener Werkstätte* was partly a by-product of the Secession. Following English models, Hoffman stressed the use of elegant modern design, perfect craftsmanship, and high quality materials for the creation of useful and beautiful objects. He declared war on the "inferior methods of mass production, . . . the mindless imitation of bygone styles" and aimed at elevating the status of the applied arts. "The work of the craftsman must be measured by the same standards as that of the painter and sculptor . . . It cannot possibly be sufficient to buy pictures, even the most beautiful, as long as our cities, our houses, our rooms, our cupboards, our utensils, our jewellery; as long as our speech and sentiments fail to express in an elegant, beautiful, and simple fashion the spirit of our times, we will continue to be immeasurably far behind our forefathers, and no amount of lies can deceive us about all these weaknesses."

It was the dream of the *Werkstätte* group to exemplify their convictions through a building which would carry their trademark. They would design everything — exterior and interior — from the gable down to the last carpet, the last chair, the last piece of cutlery. The dream came true in the building of a sanatorium in Purkersdorf on the western outskirts of Vienna, but the most ideal commission was received from Adolphe Stoclet, a Belgian millionaire who was enthusiastic about the principles of the *Werkstätte*. He wanted a building for his own use in Vienna, but Stoclet had to return to his home country. The "Viennese" building therefore stands in Brussels, and is still owned by the Stoclet family.

Musical Trends

A similar confrontation between traditional and modern ideas occured in the field of music, where innovative approaches challenged classical harmonies. The favourite composer of the Ringstraße society was Johannes Brahms. Coming from Hamburg, he explained his settling down in Vienna with the words: *Ich kann nur auf dem Dorfe arbeiten.* "I can only work in a village." His home was in the neighbourhood of the *Musikverein,* whose artistic director he was, on *Karlsplatz* where his monument can be found today. Brahms' symphonies and chamber music offered the concert-going public what they liked: classical structures interwoven with romantic emotions.

While Brahms was appreciated by the critics and applauded by the public, a man from the country, an Upper Austrian peasant type, Anton Bruckner, wrote symphonies which, because of their length and "noise," many believed to be unperformable. Eduard Hanslick, the influential critic of the *Neue Freie Presse,* the paper of the liberal establishment, anathemized Bruckner. The emperor, however, was benevolent to him.

When Bruckner was an old and sick man, Franz Joseph gave him a residence in one of the buildings adjacent to the Belvedere Palace.

One of Bruckner's admirers was the young composer and conductor Gustav Mahler. Like numerous other talents of the *fin de siècle,* Mahler was the son of Jewish immigrants from Bohemia. Just as the storming Secessionists, he was a fervent fighter for his cause, a missionary for purity in matters of musical and artistic production. His ten years as director of the Vienna Opera are called its "Golden Period" (1897–1907). Up to this time, the Opera had been more of a playground for the vanity and self-representation of the upper classes than a temple of musical perfectionism. People came not only to listen; they also wanted to be seen. Not a very agreeable boss of the house, Mahler ran it only for the sake of producing excellent opera. He ordered the lights in the audience hall to be switched off when a performance was about to begin, thus forcing latecomers to wait for a pause to take their seats. He also ruthlessly persecuted the "claque," a group singers paid to applaud which had become a semi-official institution.

Due to Mahler's demand for precision and discipline, the Vienna Opera offered a series of the most brilliant productions, particularly of operas by Richard Wagner, whose music had been the topic of endless debate among musical connoisseurs. Along with the great success, however, there were also clashes and conflicts. "What you theatre people call tradition," said Mahler, "is nothing else than laziness and sloppiness." The end was painful and unfortunate. Mahler left Vienna and went to New York where he worked as a conductor for the Metropolitan Opera. After a few years, he returned to Austria, sick and near death, and died in Vienna in 1911. It is significant that, despite his long association with the city, none of Mahler's symphonies had their world premiere in Vienna, nor did he ever conduct any of them in local concert halls.

While relatively few people appreciated the creative genius of Bruckner and Mahler, all social groupings of Vienna, from the top layer down to the masses, fell under the spell of the "Waltz King" Johann Strauß (son). He conducted waltzes for the dancing Viennese until he was ready to collapse from exhaustion. At the same time, he elevated the waltz – originally a country dance — to an orchestral concert piece. It became a classic. The waltz *At the Blue Danube* was performed for the first time in 1867 by the renowned *Wiener Männergesangsverein*. However, probably because of its first silly text, it was ill-received by the Viennese. Shortly afterwards, Strauß conducted an orchestral arrangement of this most Viennese of all his waltzes at the World Exhibition in Paris. It immediately became a hit and, together with his father's *Radetzky March,* is now an unofficial Viennese anthem. In 1876, Johann Strauß was invited to Boston to assist in the celebration of the centennial of the United States where he conducted 20,000 singers and instrumentalists.

Strauß also captured Vienna on the stage with his operettas, the most famous of which is *Die Fledermaus.* Along with Karl Millöcker, Richard Heuberger, and Franz von Suppé he made Vienna a centre of this species of musical entertainment with its easy-to-hum melodies and happy endings: *The Beggar's Student, The Opera Ball, The Gipsy Baron.* Although the topics of these operettas are no longer up-to-date, they still fill the cash boxes of the *Volksoper* and comfort the tourists during the annual summer pauses.

New Literary Horizons

In the same year Johann Strauß died and the Secession building was opened, 1899, a book was published which remained almost unnoticed. Within eight years, only 600 copies of *The Interpretation of Dreams* were sold. This is not the place to discuss breadth and depth and permanence of Sigmund Freud's work, but the fact that Vienna was the birthplace of psychoanalysis cannot be overlooked. The social and cultural environment of the city definitely contributed to the development of Freud's theory.

Freud himself regarded Arthur Schnitzler to be his "double" in the field of literature. The two never met, but they did exchange letters. One of Freud's reads: "I have the impression that you intuitively — actually as the consequence of intense

The literary coffee-house of fin de siècle Vienna: Café GrTo

The literary coffee-house of fin de siècle Vienna: Café Griensteidl

self-observation — know all things which I have discovered in other people only as a result of tedious, detailed research."

Schnitzler, like Freud a doctor, tried to uncover the inner dimensions of the people of the *Ringstraße*. His stories concern love and death, and who would not think of Vienna — the city of both theatre and psychoanalysis — when reading Schnitzler's observation: *Wir spielen alle — wer es weiß, ist klug.* "We all act; he who knows it, is clever."

Schnitzler and his literati friends met in the coffee-houses of Vienna. Up to this day, coffee-houses are not only places for loners "who prefer to be alone without being lonely," they are also meeting places. The coffee houses of the 19th century played an important role in the city. There were around 700 coffee-houses in 1904, and certain ones attracted different circles of the intelligentsia or artists. They were centres of political discussion and places for study. But, above all, they provided the setting for friendly and critical conversation. Some of the customers almost lived in the places, used their addresses for mail and laundry, and borrowed money from the waiters.

The availability of coffee, innumerable glasses of water, newspapers — an encyclopedia was even to be found in the *Café Griensteidl* — offered an environment for discussion on all the hot topics of the day. There was an especially strong and particularly Viennese interest in cultural matters: Richard Wagner's controversial operas, Mahler's operatic productions, Klimt's nudes.

Literati also wrote at their cafés. On the marble tables of the coffee-houses, they did not create voluminous novels, but rather short stories, essays and critiques — coffee-house literature. One of the most well-known of the coffee-house cliques was Hermann Bahr, a bearded father figure with a special sense for new trends in art and literature who pushed the talents of his group. The embodiment of a coffee-house customer was the impressionist poet Peter Altenberg, a hippy-like figure with unique powers of observation. Hugo von Hofmannsthal also frequented the cafés. Writing mature poetry as a high school boy, he later became a renowned Austrian author and was responsible for the text of the Viennese *Rosenkavalier*. Together with the actor Max Reinhardt, he started the projects of the Salzburg Festival.

There was one coffee-house patron who expressed his discontent with his society not only through "coffee-house literature" but also with the way he built his café. The *Café Museum*, designed by Adolf Loos in 1899, lacked the plush dark red upholstery and the twilight atmosphere of other coffee-houses in the city. Its furniture was cool and functional instead. Due to the bareness of its design, the Viennese dubbed it "Café Nihilism." Loos also shocked the public with the house he built on *Michaelerplatz*. Because it had no window mouldings, the Viennese labelled it "the house without eyebrows." However, its severity created a storm. The house vexed the emperor, who allegedly no longer used the entrance to the Hofburg on the square to avoid looking at it.

Loos' purism in architecture was an expression of his philosophy. Stepping out of his field, he also wrote biting essays criticizing the manners and customs of his cultural environment. He directed his critique not only at historicism but also at the aesthetic ambitions of the Vienna Workshops. Attacking the overabundance of historical ornamentation as well as modern decoration around him, Loos stated in the essay "Ornament and Crime": "Ornament is wasted work and therefore wasted health. That's what is always used to be. But nowadays, it also means a waste of materials and both mean waste of capital."

Perhaps the only man whose criticism surpassed Loos' acid exhortations was Karl Kraus. Another customer of the coffeehouse and another purist, Kraus had an outstanding talent for handling the German language. Like Loos, he was not born in Vienna but came from a neighbouring corner of the empire. The son of Jewish immigrants, Kraus made a frustrating attempt at becoming an actor and then turned to writing where he preached and practiced purity of language. Financially independent, he was also free from the demands and pressures of influential groups in society. He wrote his magazine, *Die Fackel* (The Torch), entirely by himself for 25 years.

Kraus was a moralist, and as Loos remarked: "His grammar book was his Bible." Through his polemics, he intended to show the moral defects in the character of other writers by unmasking their language. Keeping himself busy analysing the articles of his colleagues and the scandals of his time, Kraus knew few limits. With fanaticism he attacked the press, corruption, psychoanalysis, feminism, as well as Zionism. Consequently, he had few friends. However, his treatment and defense of the German language was a unique phenomenon, never to be repeated again.

In Vienna during the *fin de siècle* not only social critics but also architects, doctors, and painters wrote in hopes of changing the world. Seldom heard before, women now gained a voice through writing. One outstanding woman, Bertha von Suttner, attempted to give a new direction to the world through the peace movement. Her family background prescribed a career as a lady of the society — a hostess or a patroness. This is one reason why in her role as a social activist she often met with smiles and scorn. Living in Russia during the Russian-Turkish War, von Suttner had opened her home to the wounded. There she made her decision to work for peace. She wrote a book, *Die Waffen nieder* (Down with Arms), which was nothing less than a complete condemnation of war. Although it was difficult for her to find a publisher at first, once von Suttner's book was in print it became a bestseller. It was translated into all major languages and ran through 36 editions. Founding and thereafter leading the Austrian peace movement, von Suttner continued to write and lecture about peace throughout her life. In 1899, an enthusiastic reader of *Die Waffen nieder,* the Russian Tsar Nicholas II, organized the first Peace Conference in the Hague, and von Suttner participated as the only woman. In 1905, she was awarded the Nobel Peace Prize in recognition of her efforts. A blessing of sorts, she died in July 1914, a week before World War I broke out.

Another book written at the time was more successful in the long run, Theodor Herzl's *Der Judenstaat* (The Jewish State). Herzl's experiences with anti-semitism in Vienna and as correspondent for the *Neue Freie Presse* in Paris generated many of the ideas he developed in his book. He advocated the foundation of a state where Jews who neither were willing to assimilate nor endure persecution could find a home land.

In some circles, particularly within the Jewish establishment in Vienna, the book was met with rejection and mockery. The *Neue Freie Presse,* which had Jews on the staff and many Jewish readers, never printed the word "Zionism." In other areas however, Herzl was successful. Restlessly propagating his cause, he sought aid from foreign leaders and monarchs and organized six Zionist World Congresses between 1897 and his death in 1904. David Ben Gurion, the famous Israeli politician, called Herzl a unique combination of a theoretician and a pragmatist. Forty-five years after Herzl's death, Israel was created. The Jews had to endure the Holocaust before Herzl's dream could be realized.

The Influence of Viennese Schools

It would be unfair to speak only of the great individuals and the dreams and projects dreamt and designed in studios or coffee-houses. The various "schools" called "Viennese" should be mentioned as well; their discoveries and teachings exercise global influence up to this day.

During the second half of the 19th century the Medical School of Vienna became world renowned. The work of Karl

A surgical pioneer, Theodor Billroth (1829-94)

von Rokitansky, Josef Hyrtl and Joseph Skoda — just to mention a few — revolutionized the field of diagnostics while Clemens von Pirquet pioneered in the study of the allergies. Ferdinand von Hebra did the same for skin deseases; Theodor Billroth from Hamburg introduced new surgical techniques; Robert Bárány won the Nobel Prize for his research on ear ailments as did Julius von Wagner-Jauregg for his work in psychiatry. A "saviour of mothers" Ignaz Philipp Semmelweis, fought puerperal fever. Vienna was a Mecca for doctors and medical students. In 1895—96 extra courses were opened for American doctors. After a few years, the American Medical Association assumed responsibility for organizing advanced medical training programmes. It brought 21,000 American doctors to Vienna between 1904 and 1921.

Outside the medical establishment, Freud met with his students every Wednesday evening in his office in the *Berggasse*.

These private meetings were the beginning of the so-called school of psychoanalysis. Some of Freud's students developed the principles of the master's theories in new directions, but their achievements are often underestimated. Alfred Adler, the father of individual psychology, is most famous for coining the term "inferiority complex," but his greatest achievement was to add a social dimension to the treatment of neuroses. Child guidance clinics in the English speaking world in particular are a living testimony to his teachings.

The Austrian school of economics, which also exerts a great deal of influence in the English speaking world, had its origins in Vienna as well. The founding fathers, Karl Menger, Eugen von Böhm-Bawerk, Friedrich von Wieser, developed the theory of marginal value. They have influenced following generations of economists as well as political theorists and sociologists throughout the world.

Hans Kelsen, a legal theoretician, also contributed to Viennese influences in the social sciences. Responsible for the drafting of the constitution of the Austrian republic in 1920 and contributing to the Charter of the United Nations, Kelsen's pure theory of law challenged conventional assumptions and exercised global influence.

There were also innovations in the humanities. The University of Vienna was the first institution in the world to teach art history as an independent discipline. New methods of analysis and interpretation, similar to a scientific approach, belonged to the foundations for the Viennese school of art history, representatives of which still can be found abroad today.

It is an interesting phenomenon that the city as an intellectual centre experienced a climax just before the demise of the Habsburg Empire which had been responsible for Vienna's importance and radiance. Tensions and confrontations as well as political and social transformations certainly contributed to this creativity, which was also indeed inspired by disharmony and friction. *Fin de siècle* artists and intellectuals turned away from their historical environment; they broke out of traditional ruts of thought and away from patterns appreciated and followed by the majority. In some cases part of the reason for their new vistas might have been personal. A number of them were immigrants and therefore not fully integrated into society.

Frustration or aggression and ambition may have combined to push them toward new parameters in art and thought.

Looking at intellectual and artistic accomplishments, the end of the era was effervescent. Vienna hardly ever amplified new trends; on the contrary, it rather muted them. Great contemporaries seldom received public adulation. However, there are a tremendous number of monuments and memorials in the city indicating that in Vienna the present must become the past before it is accepted.

VIII. The Imperial Capital Becomes a Socialist Stronghold

On June 28, 1914, Archduke Franz Ferdinand, the heir to Franz Joseph, was assassinated during an official visit to Sarajevo. A young Serbian nationalist shot him and his wife at point-blank range. One month later, the aged emperor signed a declaration of war on the small Balkan state of Serbia, which had been accused of harbouring the assassins, and began the First World War. He did not live long enough to experience the bitterness of defeat and the deterioration of his empire. His death on November 21, 1916 ended a 68 year reign, and the passing of this sign of stability was an omen of things to come. Franz Joseph's successor, Karl I, inherited the crown and a hopeless situation. He wanted to get Austria-Hungary out of the war and attempted to placate the empire's national minorities with promises of reorganization and autonomy, but his efforts were too timid and came too late.

The centrifugal forces of nationlism tore the war-weary empire apart. Woodrow Wilson's Fourteen Points became the basis for claims to national self-determination, and Czeckoslovakian and Yugoslavian proclamations of independence began the dismemberment of the empire. Poland re-emerged as a state after over a century of partition under Austrian, German, and Russian rule, and sundry peripheral territories were lost to Rumania. A new border with Italy was not drawn along the promised "clearly recognizable lines of nationality." On the contrary, 250,000 South Tyroleans, German speaking Austrians, were sacrificed to give Italy control of the strategically important Brenner Pass. The German speaking Austrians in Czechoslovakia suffered a similar fate. The Czechs claimed and were granted the historical borders of the provinces of Bohemia and Moravia which stranded 3,000,000 so-called *Sudetendeutsche* inside of the new national borders. Austria and Hun-

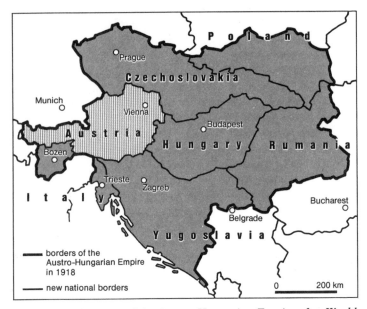

The dismemberment of the Austro-Hungarian Empire after World War I

gary, the pillars of the Dual Monarchy, became entirely separate and truncated states.

Vienna was naturally the scene of the most important events. After the empire began to fall apart, the German speaking representatives from the *Reichsrat,* the multinational imperial parliament which dealt with the domestic affairs for the Austrian half of the monarchy, formed a provisional national assembly on October 21, 1918. Karl I renounced his responsibility for state affairs on November 12 ending 640 years of Habsburg rule. On the same day, the Republic of German-Austria was proclaimed from the ramp of the Parliament to jubilant masses, but not all of the Viennese were enthusiastic. The transition from a monarchy to a republic and from an empire to a small state shattered a world-view, a traditional social order, and an established way of life.

*The proclamation of the Republic of German-Austria from the ramp
of the Parliament on November 12, 1918*

Off to a Bad Start

The proclamation of German-Austria was an attempt by
the German speaking politicians from the Austrian half of the
empire to exercise national self-determination. The name
German-Austria was chosen because "Austria" at that time
had imperial and multinational connotations. The provisional
government under the chancellorship of a moderate socialist,
Dr. Karl Renner, assumed the task of breaking with the past
and creating a state. In 1919, a special "Habsburg Law" was
passed banning from Austria members of the Habsburg family
who refused to take an oath of allegiance to the republic. It
also nationalized their property and made the public use of
aristocratic titles as well as the noble prefix *von* illegal. Karl I
died in exile in 1922, and his family could not return to Austria to bury him with his predecessors in the *Kaisergruft*. (His
aged wife, Empress Zita, returned to Austria for the first

time in 1983, and the Viennese received her with a mixture of curiosity and nostalgia.)

Very few people, the politicians included, actually believed in the viability of a small, German speaking, Austrian state. The proclamation of the First Republic included an article which stated that Austria was to enter a political union *(Anschluß)* with Germany, but the victorious powers forbade this. In 1919, the Treaty of St. Germain was dictated to Austria. The Austrian peace delegation went to France to negotiate, but its president, Renner, was subjected to the humiliation of having to wait in an antechamber for the terms. After governmental and parliamentary consultation, the terms of the treaty were accepted under protest. German-Austria was to be called Austria, and this small state was burdened with reparations for the Habsburg's war.

Austrians hardly identified with their newly formed republican mini-state. Many of them either had political leanings towards Germany or identified with stronger and older provincial traditions. Old monarchists scorned the republicans. The virtual absence of a national identity and a lack of confidence in the viability of the state plagued Austria from its inception on. The Viennese in particular were accustomed to viewing their city and themeselves in grander political dimensions. The "Imperial and Royal Capital and Residence," the centre of an empire with 52 million inhabitants, had become the over-sized capital of a small state of just over 6 million practically overnight. The city lost the role it was designed to play. Stranded on the easternmost tip of the Alps, it was effectively isolated from the state it was to rule.

The relationship of Vienna to the new-born state of Austria was often compared to hydrocephalus, a rare disease which causes the head of infants to swell completely out of proportion to their bodies. In German, this condition is commonly called *Wasserkopf* or "waterhead." This term was popularly applied to Vienna because practically every third Austrian lived there. The provinces — as the body which had to support this over-sized "waterhead" — traditionally had a strained relationship to Vienna. To this very day, some Viennese colloquially refer to people from the provinces as *G'scherte*: a reference to the sheared *(geschert)* heads of 18th century farmers who could easily be identified as country bumpkins. This traditional and structural incompatibility was also reinforced by ideological hostility; the provinces were conservative and Vienna became a socialist stronghold. Even today a rather ambivalent relationship exists between Vienna and the provinces although the intensity of the feelings involved has dissipated.

Immediately after the war, the Viennese found themselves in a desparate situation. The newly formed neighbouring states hermetically sealed their borders with Austria. Today the two main rail terminals in Vienna are the West and the South Stations, but in 1914 the most important of the six rail terminals were the North and the East Stations. This shows to what extent Vienna was economically oriented towards the former empire. Coal, for example, previously came from areas which were incorporated into Southern Poland. Czechoslovakia was an important industrial area, and foodstuffs came from the agricultural expanses of the Hungarian Plain. Suppliers and markets disappeared, which caused many businesses to close down, and unemployment skyrocketed as a result. Food also was not being delivered from its former sources, and the farmers from the Austrian provinces hesitated to send their goods to Vienna because they traditionally had other markets and really could only expect worthless currency in return. Inflation soared to astronomical heights and destroyed savings. In 1919, one US dollar was worth nine crowns; by 1922 it could buy 83,000 crowns. The introduction of the *Schilling* in 1924 finally brought this situation under control.

Hunger, epidemic illness, and tuberculosis ravaged the Viennese population. Infant mortality rose to 25%, and the Viennese began to cut down trees in the Vienna Woods for fuel. Soldiers returning from the front found unemployment and practically nothing else. The state released tens of thousands of bureaucrats who had so faithfully served the emperor and the empire, and a peculiar kind of upper class poverty appeared as a result. The wives of bureaucrats, who often had held important positions in the administration of the far-flung territories of the empire, bartered with jewels, furs, rugs, and the family silver until absolutely nothing was left.

The collapse of the empire not only changed Vienna's economic position but also its political landscape. Universal male

Part of the Vienna Woods in 1919; the lack of coal turned this recreational area into a source of heating material

and female suffrage was introduced, and the first truly free and democratic municipal elections in Vienna resulted in a clear victory for the Social Democrats who polled 60% of the votes. They built their programmes upon the foundations provided by the reforms of Karl Lueger but also assumed a much more progressive political course. Vienna was the first major city in the world to have a socialist administration, and since 1919 every freely elected *Bürgermeister* (mayor) and the majority of the City Council have been socialist. The socialist administration of Vienna became an internationally recognized model for health, welfare, and housing programmes.

The drafting and ratification of the Austrian constitution in 1920 also effected the status of Vienna. The city was designated federal capital and given the option of becoming a province in its own right. Up until then, Vienna had been a city in and the capital of Lower Austria. Its advancement to provincial status actually robbed Lower Austria of its historical capital, and to this day the main government offices for Lower Austria are located in Vienna's *Herrengasse*. The greatest political advantage of the separation of Vienna from Lower Austria was legislative autonomy not to mention the fact that taxes could be levied and federal funds be drawn on two levels, as a city and a province. The electoral success of the Social Democrats and the constitutionally anchored political autonomy of Vienna provided the basis for 15 years of socialist administration which was cursed and praised as *Rotes Wien* (Red Vienna). The separation of Vienna from Lower Austria also had its advantages from the conservative point of view. A dangerous "red virus" had been isolated within the new provincial borders.

Old and New Cultures

Vienna, the big city, and Social Democracy were just one pole of Austrian political life; the other was represented by the provinces, agriculture, traditionalism, and the Catholicism of the Christian Social movement. The conservatives supported by several small middle class parties controlled the provinces and the federal Parliament; the Social Democrats were a minority in opposition and held Vienna as an isolated stronghold. The philosophy behind the programmes of social reform which the Social Democrats introduced in Vienna was called Austro-Marxism. The Austro-Marxists rejected violence as a means of social change, yet they were convinced that the victory of democracy would enable the masses to peacefully establish socialism. This commitment to democratic *and* revolutionary principles was summarized by Otto Bauer, a leading theoretician and the chairman of the Social Democratic Party, in a simple motto: "Don't crack their skulls; win their minds." The political rhetoric of Austro-Marxists — revolution, class struggle, building socialism — may have obscured their commitment to democracy. However, their commitment to democracy hindered them from making any violent attempts to put the revolutionary rhetoric into practice. In any case, Austro-Marxism represented a threat to established and traditional conservative Viennese values.

The Austro-Marxist idea of revolutionary change went far beyond the traditional working class party concerns of labour conditions, wages, and social security and included education, art, sexuality, sports, and all forms of leisure. Socialism was understood as an encompassing alternative to the traditional, bourgeois, capitalistic way of life. The idea of *Arbeiterkultur,* workers' or proletarian culture, aimed at nothing less than creating a new society based on socialist values and principles of organization, and Red Vienna was regarded as a prototype and a radical new cultural beginning. Workers' culture resulted in the proliferation of socialist organizations: youth groups, hiking and automobile clubs, athletic teams, theatre groups, etc., some of which exist to date. The positive attempt to instill the working classes with their own cultural institutions and identity had the negative side effect of extending political polarization from the level of party politics into practically every realm of life. Even though workers' culture in some cases merely imitated bourgeois traditions, it marks the establishment of a new anti-traditional culture. This was the beginning of a "second" Vienna based on the idea of really being able to change the existing social order.

Workers' culture accompanied its members from the cradle to the grave. The Vienna Health Office gave the mothers of newborn children a clothing package, which is still incidentally distributed today, so that enough diapers and fresh laundry were available at least at the start, and health services dropped the child mortality rate drastically. There was also a special organization called *Die Flamme* (The Flame) whose over 100,000 members were dedicated to cremation. A striking contrast to the traditional Viennese funeral ritual, cremation was a pointed anti-religious and anti-clerical gesture which many socialists interpreted as a sign of progress. The erection of a crematory near the *Zentralfriedhof* (Central Cemetery) in 1923 caused a public scandal because municipal funds were used to support something Roman Catholics then regarded as sacrilegious. Workers' culture had high aspirations, but the polarized political situation condemned it to the status of a sub-culture which the established Viennese scorned and feared.

Many long standing Viennese cultural institutions and traditions survived the collapse of the Empire more or less intact. The court *(Hof)* theatres *(Oper* and *Burgtheater),* which had been privately subsidized by the emperor, became state theatres — hence the State Opera — and the stat's responsibility for these extremely popular and deficitory institutions was anchored in the federal constitution. Theatrical and musical traditions continued with an almost unbroken vitality. In the midst of the worst post-war misery, Richard Strauss and Hugo von Hofmannsthal collaborated on *Die Frau ohne Schatten* which premièred at the State Opera in October, 1919. Viennese authors like Karl Kraus, Joseph Roth, and Hugo von Hofmannsthal created a series of literary masterpieces which critically or nostalgically attempted to articulate the loss of the empire.

In his study in the *Berggasse* in the 9th district, Freud continued the lonely work on his theory of psychoanalysis. He was conscientiously neglected by the Viennese medical community which continued to build up the reputation of the Vienna School of Medicine. Ludwig Wittgenstein and members of a group of philosophers called the Vienna Circle laid important parts of the foundations of modern analytical philosophy. Adolf Loos worked for Vienna's communal building office.

Vienna, a city of great musical traditions and traditional musical tastes, was also one of the birthplaces of modern music. Arnold Schönberg and Joseph Matthias Hauer revolutionized composing by developing the 12 tone system. Replacing the traditional tonal system with an entirely new concept of musical form, they exercised global influence as the fathers of the "New Vienna School of Music." One of Schönberg's students, Alban Berg, composed in a simliar vein. Berg's atonal opera *Wozzek* had its Viennese premiere in 1927. Another 12 tone composer, Anton von Webern, also conducted some of the symphonic concerts which were especially organized for the working class.

The creative fermentation which had begun after the construction of the *Ringstraße* and before the end of the empire continued in interwar Vienna, but in spite of political, artistic, and intellectual innovations many Viennese maintained their long-standing preferences. Traditionalism and innovation met head on in the arts as well as in politics.

Red Vienna

The financial basis for the realization of Red Vienna's manifold social welfare programmes was created by a revolution in the system of taxation. To redistribute the tax burden, the socialists propagated the now commonplace but then radical idea of direct and progressive taxation. Charges for municipal services like transportation and water were lowered along with the taxes on necessities, and new taxes were introduced on property and luxury goods like automobiles, horses, dogs, servants, and certain foods and drinks. In addition to this, the *Wohnbausteuer*, a new tax on rents which went into the municipal building fund, came into effect. The working class renters of small, substandard apartments, 82% of the taxed households, paid only 22% of the total taxes collected; the renters of 3,426 "luxury" objects, a mere 0.5% of the tax base, contributed 45% to the total.

Many of Vienna's social welfare programmes were the initiative of Julius Tandler, an anatomist who was the City Councilman for Health. True to his motto, "he who builds children palaces, tears prison walls down," Tandler was responsible for founding many kindergartens, children's swimming pools, school dental clinics, noon meals at schools, and 35 branches of the *Mutterberatungsstelle*, an office where social workers helped mothers with problems. He also established an institute for cancer research and new and better facilities for the treatment of tuberculosis. Vienna consequently developed a reputation as the "Mecca of social welfare."

Many social programmes were directly or indirectly related to the long standing Viennese problem of housing. In 1917, renter protection *(Mieterschutz)* had been introduced by imperial decree in order to protect the families and flats of soldiers who were on the front. *Mieterschutz* froze rents and prevented arbitrary evictions. The Social Democrats managed to anchor renter protection in the laws of the First Republic where it assumed a completely different role. Post-war inflation effectively reduced the rents people paid as well as the profits landlords made. Although the working classes benefited greatly from renter protection, it also discouraged private investment in residential building at a time when there was a tremendous housing shortage. Remaining a primary point of contention between the Social Democrats and the Christian Socials throughout the First Republic, renter protection has survived to date in a modified, less controversial, but nevertheless renter friendly form.

Mieterschutz helped improve the financial situation of the working classes, but it was a defensive measure in comparison to the offensive of communal residential building projects, the *Gemeindebauten*. These projects were planned and owned by the city which financed them from the funds provided by the revised tax system. Designed by 200 different architects working as individuals and groups, the projects varied in size. Most of the large projects, the so-called superblocks, were in the traditional working class districts on the periphery of the city where there was room for large scale development.

The city planners had a finite amount of money and space at their disposal and tens of thousands of needy families. This simple fact influenced the design of the *Gemeindebauten*; instead of building fewer, larger apartments, more smaller flats were erected. Many of the municipal apartments were hardly larger than the infamous *Bassena* flats, but they represented an enormous improvement in living standards. An average unit had a small entryway, running water and a toilet, luxuries which some Viennese flats do not have to date, a kitchen, a smaller and a larger room, as well as gas and electricity.

The buildings were designed to give the living quarters as much fresh air and natural light as possible — rickets was another common childhood affliction in Vienna — and as a rule, they only covered 40 to 60% of the lots on which they were built instead of the 85% allowed by building codes. This had ruthlessly been exploited by private builders in the past who had attempted to squeeze the greatest number of apartments into the smallest amount of space. Balconies were a common feature, and the large courtyards which resulted from this type of design doubled as playgrounds and parks. In the larger projects, the courtyards often housed a common laundry or social services provided by the city like kindergartens, dental clinics, libraries, and bathing facilities. Showers were not originally included in the *Gemeindebauten* because they would have been taxed as luxuries. (The City of Vienna still runs some

Part of the middle tract of the Reumanhof, a communal housing project built on the Margaretengürtel during 1924—25

public bathing facilities which is a good indication of the amount of substandard housing which still exists.) Last but not least, rents were low, maximally 8% of an average worker's monthly wages, apartments were assigned according to need, and the needy were predominantly Social Democrats or politically so inclined. The *Gemeindebau* projects were also effectively a public works programme to keep down unemployment. Their construction provided jobs for many of the people who were to live in the municipal housing.

The sober, geometrically designed facades so characteristic of the *Gemeindebauten* are the result of aesthetic and financial considerations. On the one hand, the municipal building authorities had set up a series of building restrictions. Windows, doors, apartment sizes, etc., were normed, and the costs of construction were closely calculated. This limited the freedom of the architects to a certain extent, but, on the other hand, they were interested in building modern. Some of the architects were students of Wagner as well as representatives of the new style of functionalism. Decoration was held to a minimum, and ornamentation often involved the spartanic depiction of socialist heroes or working class themes, the backbones of workers' culture. The city patronized artists and sculptors with these projects.

From 1923 to 1933, communal building projects produced 63,000 residental units, new homes for over 220,000 people. Twenty six of the 384 apartment complexes had over 800 individual units and were symptomatic for the classical *Gemeindebau* superblock style. One of the largest superblocks was physically and ideologically monumental; from 1927–30, 1,382 apartments for over 5,000 people were erected in *Heiligenstadt* in the 19th district. The *Karl Marx Hof* was built on a narrow lot almost a kilometer long. The length of the facade spans three streetcar stops.

Without a doubt, the communal building programme was ideological and political in intent. It was a solution to the housing problem as well as an alternative to private property. Apart from their aesthetic objections, conservative critics saw the *Gemeindebauten* as conglomerations of Marxist fanatics, symbols of collectivization, and fortresses which were being strategically placed throughout the city as part of a plan to overthrow the state. An explanation is necessary to clarify this last accusation in particular, and it will simultaneously illustrate the political climate in which RedVienna existed.

Fortress Mentalities

One of the unfortunate characteristics of the domestic politics of the First Republic was the existence of armed political organizations. In the chaos of 1918 when the state was in the process of being formed, various citizens' defense organizations were founded to compensate for the virtual absence of any police or executive powers. In the country, these groups were called *Heimwehr* (home defense) and did exactly what their name says. They protected their villages, families, and property, often from marauding soldiers returning from the front, and in border regions like Burgenland, Styria, and Carinthia, they defended Austrian territory against invasions by foreign neighbours who aspired to change the borders by force. In the cities, the workers organized to protect utilities and factories, helped maintain public order, and held the communists in check. Armed Social Democratic workers spoiled a communist putsch attempt in 1919. Both of these armed self-defense organizations outlived their original usefulness and unfortunately became permanent fixtures of domestic politics.

The *Heimwehr* was to a great extent aligned with the Christian Socials, and the Social Democrats formed a sub-organization called the *Republikanischer Schutzbund* (Republican Defense League) dedicated to defending the constitution against any violent attempts from the left or the right to undermine it. It also provided for security and order at socialist meetings, marches, and rallies. In other words, there were two politically opposed private armies in Austria. Both were armed with weapons and suspicion and defensively prepared for their enemies to attempt to overthrow the constitutional order. For the conservatives, therefore, the *Gemeindebauten* were not figurative fortresses but real ones: strategically placed, easily defensible positions for the *Schutzbund.* There is no evidence indicating that the socialist municipal administration chose building sites or designed buildings strategically, but it was a simple matter of fact that the larger complexes housed large numbers of *Schutzbund* members. For some, the *Gemeindebauten* were monumental symbols of workers' culture; for others they were signs of danger and subversion.

In January, 1927, members of the *Schutzbund* and their conservative counterparts had, as was often the case with these weekend soldiers, a confrontation in the small village of Schattendorf in Burgenland. Unlike most of these politically inspired confrontations, which ended harmlessly, this one ended fatally. After a typical altercation, members of a veterans' club fired into a crowd of *Schutzbund* members and supporters, killing a war invalid and an eight year old child, and wounding five others. Three men were put on trail for murder in Vienna and acquitted on July 14, 1927. The accused maintained to have acted in self-defense which, given the evidence, was not popularly accepted, and the rank and file socialists were enraged that "workers' murderers" had been acquitted. The leadership of the Social Democratic Party felt that it would be unwise to protest the results of a jury trial and therefore avoided discussing the entire question with the indignant rank and file. Fired up by an aggressive lead article in the party's official newspaper, *Arbeiter-Zeitung,* the workers took things into their own hands.

The next day, a spontaneous demostration took place without the authorization of party leadership or party coordination and discipline. Thousands of protesters left work, assembled on the Ring near the *Rathaus* and the Parliament, and each attempt of the police to master the situation by force resulted in an escalation of aggression and violence on both sides. Mounted police with swords tried to break up the unorganized protesters. Thousands of demonstrators were driven away from the Parliament and gathered in the adjoining park in front of the Palace of Justice which arbitrarily became the victim of their aggressions.

The building was set on fire, the rage of the protesters started to ebb, and lemonade salesmen appeared on the scene to do business. The crowd refused to let the fire department through to extinguish the flames even though socialist politicians hurried over from their offices in the *Rathaus* and begged them to cooperate. The conservative federal government did not think that the Viennese authorities had the situation under control and gave the police permission to use fire arms to reestablish order. The police fired into the crowd repeatedly. The day ended with 89 dead and 1,057 wounded; only four of the fatalities were police. The conservative government was just as indignant about the violence of the "mob" as the Social Democrats were about the governmentally sanctioned violence of the police against unarmed civilians. The Social Democrats completely lost their confidence in the government, the police, and the Christian Socials who, in turn, began to take a much more authoritarian attitude towards the "problem" which the Social Democrats represented. The will to cooperate with each other disappeared, and a more militant tone entered into politics.

133

The Violent End

The Great Depression hit Vienna hard. The *Creditanstalt* with its main office at *Schottentor* was one of the first continental banks to start floundering. Unemployment rose rapidly creating yet another political controversy, and Austrian democracy deteriorated along with the Austrian economy. During a very turbulent session in Parliament on March 4, 1933, all three "presidents" — the parliamentary officers responsible for presiding over the sessions — resigned. This left the Parliament with a problem not covered by its rules of order or anticipated by the political parties; there was no one to call it to order or adjourn it. Instead of showing some type of democratic understanding, the conservative federal chancellor, Engelbert Dollfuß, took advantage of this situation. Declaring that Parliament had "suspended itself," he used an outdated emergency powers act from 1917 as a pseudo-legal basis for ending parliamentary democracy in Austria.

Within three months, Dollfuß banned the *Schutzbund,* which merely forced it underground, formed an organization for all supporters of his anti-democratic and authoritarian policies called the Fatherland Front, and outlawed the communist and Nazi parties in Austria. Dollfuß' ideology is called Austrofascism by some because he propagated the radically new idea of Austrian cultural, political, and national independence from Germany and combined this with certain characteristics of other fascist ideologies: authoritarian leadership, a one party system, corporate model of society, and anti-Marxism. But unlike his arch-enemy Hitler or his friend and supporter Mussolini, Dollfuß was not able to win broad popular support. With his Austrianism he merely further alienated the pro-German elements in the population, who became increasingly pro-Nazi, and with his fascism he furthered the isolation of the Social Democrats who had won 41% of the votes in the election of 1930 and were the largest party in Parliament.

The Social Democrats literally had their backs to the wall. Parliament had been circumvented, encroachments were made on civil rights, and the Dollfuß regime was still pushing hard. The question of when and how to resist was often discussed in Vienna, but the decision to resist was made independently by a

February, 1934; artillery aimed at the Karl Marx Hof

Schutzbund leader in Linz on February 12, 1934. Police surrounded a Social Democratic workers' club where they suspected hidden weapons, broke down the doors, and the *Schutzbund* opened fire. This isolated incident started an armed conflict which spread throughout Austria and lasted three days. It is apparent from the lack of preparation and coordination that the Social Democrats had not planned a revolt, but now they had to fight.

Some of the heaviest fighting was in Vienna. Pockets of resistance formed around the larger *Gemeindebauten* in the outer, predominantly working class districts: *Floridsdorf, Simmering, Meidling, Ottakring,* and the *Karl Marx Hof* in *Heiligenstadt*. Although these socialist neighbourhoods were isolated from each other and the *Schutzbund* was poorly armed as well as outnumbered, the government and *Heimwehr* forces met fierce resistance. Dollfuß' advisors encouraged him to use

135

artillery to break the morale of the *Schutzbund* because storming the individual apartment complexes with infantry would be too time consuming and bloody, and he made the militarily wise and politically catastrophic decision to do so. Artillery was brought into position against the *Gemeindebauten* and used on the *Schutzbund* members as well as women and children.

By February 15, the fighting had ended, and according to government statistics there were hundreds of dead and wounded on both sides. The losses of the *Schutzbund* actually may have been over 1,000. Karl Seitz, the mayor of Vienna, was arrested and replaced by a conservative appointee. Many leading Social Democrats fled the country, and those who remained faced trial, imprisonment, and in some cases execution. The Social Democratic Party was banned, and Red Vienna came to a violent end. The facades of the *Gemeindebauten*, torn open by artillerly and perforated with bullet holes, were repaired, but the events surrounding February, 1934, did practically irreparable damage to the political fabric of the city and the state. The fratricide has in many respects never been forgotten.

IX. The Nazi Interlude:
Vienna, Germany

On the first page of *Mein Kampf*, Hitler's autobiographical outline of Nazi ideology, he stated one of his political goals: "German-Austria must return to the great German mother country." With Hitler's rise to power in 1933, the possibility of a forceful unification of Austria with Nazi Germany, an *Anschluß*, became imminent. In Austria, Engelbert Dollfuß had unsuccessfully attempted to eliminate his opponents on the left and the right, the Communists and Social Democrats here and the Nazis there. Dollfuß had far-reaching plans for creating a new Austrian state and reforming society, but Austrian Nazis violently interrupted his vision on July 25, 1934. During a premature and poorly organized attempt to overthrow the regime, Austrian Nazis occupied the Federal Chancellor's Office on *Ballhausplatz*. Dollfuß was wounded in the process and left to bleed to death in spite of his pleas for a doctor and a priest.

The Nazis first bid for power failed miserably. Dollfuß has since remained a controversial figure. For some conservatives, he was an Austrian patriot and martyr. Viewed from the other end of the political spectrum, he was a workers' murderer and fascist who destroyed Austrian democracy. An accurate appraisal of him is somewhere in between these extremes.

Dollfuß' successor, Kurt von Schuschnigg, inherited a precarious political situation. Nazi Germany became more and more demanding, and even though the Nazi Party was illegal in Austria, its members became more and more brazen. Schuschnigg was caught between the open agitation of Austrian Nazis and the passive resistance of the Social Democrats; his domestic support was extremely limited. Forty-one percent of the population had voted for the Social Democrats in the last free elections in 1930, and even though reliable statistics are not available, the Schuschnigg regime estimated that approximately 25—30% of the population were Nazi sympathizers in 1938.

In early 1938, Austro-German relations reached a critical point. In order to consolidate his position in Austria and to prove to the world that Austria wanted to be independent from Germany, Schuschnigg announced plans for a pro-Austrian plebiscite in early March: *Ja zu Österreich!* This merely provoked Hitler into action. Attempts within Austria to create a unified front of resistance against the Nazi threat came too late and the ideological concessions which needed to be made were, in the final analysis, too great. Threatened by Nazi Germany with the bloodshed of an invasion, Schuschnigg resigned on March 11, 1938. Arthur Seyss-Inquart, a prominent Austrian Nazi who was executed after the Nuremburg Trials for war crimes he had committed as a Nazi appointee in Holland, formed a short-lived Austrian Nazi government, and Nazi Germany occupied Austria without firing a shot. Mexico was the only country to immediately lodge a formal diplomatic complaint.

The Anschluß

Hitler's decision to occupy Austria was made on a short-term basis, but it fit into his long range plans. The public reaction to the presence of German troops was overwhelmingly positive, and the jubilant welcome Hitler received upon re-entering his childhood home of Linz, merely reinforced the wisdom of his decision to occupy Austria and integrate it into the German Reich. Hitler did not reach Vienna until March 15, but his secret police and security forces flew in on the morning of the 12th prepared with lists for the work they had to do, arresting thousands of opponents of National Socialism.

Hitler had spent part of his youth (1907—13) in Vienna, and the political and social environment of the city exercised a lasting influence on him. In *Mein Kampf,* Hitler pathetically referred to this period as his "years of study and suffering in Vienna," which proved to be crucial in terms of the development of his ideology:

138

March 15, 1938; Hitler addressing the Viennese on Heldenplatz

"Vienna was and remained for me the hardest, though most thorough, school of my life. I had set foot in this town while still half a boy, and I left it a man, grown quiet and grave. In it I obtained a political view in particular which I only needed to supplement in detail, but which never left me . . . I do not know what my attitude towards the Jews, Social Democracy, or rather Marxism as a whole, the social question, etc., would be today if at such an early time the pressure of destiny — and my own study — had not built up a basic stock of personal opinions within me."

His re-entry into Vienna was a personal as well as a political triumph. The streets through which his motorcade passed were packed with spectators anxious for a glimpse of the *Führer*. He stayed in the Hotel Imperial on the Ring which had housed many visiting heads of state.

On March 15, 1938, Hitler addressed the Viennese from the balcony of the *Neue Hofburg*. Almost a quarter of a million people collected below him on *Heldenplatz,* and he outlined a new mission for Austria: "The oldest Eastern province of the German people, should, from this point on, be the newest bastion of the German Reich . . . With history as a witness, I now proclaim the entry of my homeland into the German Reich." The fact that Hitler's speech was so well attended and enthusiastically received is a source of embarassment for some Viennese. Hitler's triumphant arrival and his speech on Heldenplatz were among the greatest political spectacles Vienna ever saw. The Viennese have a renowned weakness for theatre and theatrics. Some people just came for the show, but others viewed the *Führer* and the Reich as psychological replacements for the loss of the emperor and the empire in 1918. Undoubtedly many of the Viennese on *Heldenplatz* were there because they felt "German," and there certainly were a fair number of long-standing or recently converted Nazis in the crowd, too. After all, Hitler accomplished what the post-World War I treaties with Austria and Germany had forbidden; he unified *das deutsche Volk.* The charisma and the cult of the Führer also were drawing attractions. There were many reasons for being there which is by no means an apologetic analysis. Just like the leading politicians throughout the free world, the man on the street in Vienna viewed Hitler differently in 1938 than he did in 1939, 1943 or 1945.

In spite of the absence on any real international protest, the Nazis recognized the necessity of legitimizing the *Anschluß,* and they organized a plebiscite for this purpose. The propaganda leading up to the plebiscite was particularly massive in Red Vienna because the Nazis attempted to convince the Social Democratic working classes that National Socialism was better than Marxian socialism or that belonging to the German *Volk* was more important than allegiance to the international class of the proletariate. The Nazis organized soup lines and other relief measures designed to give the Viennese a feeling for the prosperity, generosity, and security of the Reich. They also reduced unemployment rapidly. The Nazi's massive propaganda of national, racial, and cultural unification, *Ein Volk, ein Reich, ein Führer,* merely disguised the military and economic importance of the *Anschluß.* Nazi Germany needed Austrian manpower for its military forces as well as natural resources, oil and steel in particular, for its war industry. The entire gold reserves of the Austrian National Bank, 91 tons, were completely transferred to Berlin.

The Nazi plebiscite on April 10, 1938 resulted in an overwhelming affirmation of the *Anschluß*. Over 99.7% of those who voted marked *Ja* on their ballots. This creates the impression that Austria had become a Nazi stronghold overnight, but a closer examination of the circumstances reveals a different picture. During March and April, 1938, the Nazis arrested over 50,000 Austrians, and the first transport of prisoners, which included many leading politicians, left for Dachau on April 1. In Vienna, 230,000 citizens (18% of the elligible voters) were excluded from voting for political or racial reasons. Many of these people were Jewish who were denied their civil rights because the disciriminatory legislation of the Reich was applied in Austria. The reasons for voting *Ja* were even more diverse than those for attending Hitler's speech on *Heldenplatz*. Not everyone was convinced that the ballots were really secret. Fear, propaganda, illusions, real convictions, varying expectations, discrimination, and police terror provided an optimal result which surpassed even the highest Nazi expectations.

Emigration and Reorganization

Austria disappeared from the map and was named the *Ostmark*. In 1942, the *Ostmark* was organized into the *Alpen- und Donau-Reichsgaue* (Reich's Alpine and Danube Provinces). These nominal changes reflected a Nazi policy which intended to destroy Austria's cultural identity as well as every trace of former political independence. The *Anschluß* represented a violent end to the Viennese cultural tradition which had survived the collapse of the Austro-Hungarian Empire more or less intact. Many artists, intellectuals, and scientists emigrated to the West for political and racial reasons: Sigmund Freud and his daughter, Anna; the composer, Schönberg; the conductor, Bruno Walter; the economist, von Mises; the Nobel Prize winning physicist, Schrödinger; the philosophers of the Vienna Circle; authors like Zweig, Werfel, Musil, and Torberg; Max

Reinhardt of theatre fame; the film producer and director Otto Preminger; and the list of this brain drain could go on and on. These emigrants spread out all over the world. The fact that many of them did not return to Austria after the war represents a great cultural loss for Vienna, on the one hand, but a gain of influence for Viennese schools of thought throughout the world, on the other.

Many who did not or could not emigrate were ostracized, imprisoned, or died in concentration camps. The Nazis categorically excluded Jews from participating in all forms of public life: politics, civil service, education, medicine, law, and the arts. Works of Jewish artists, composers, and authors, as well as others who did not conform to rigid Nazi cultural standards, could not be displayed, performed, or even sold. The heavy hand of Nazi segregation and censorship completely changed the cultural environment of the city. For example, the works of Gustav Mahler disappeared from concert programs because he was a Jew. The official culture was *deutsche Kultur.*

Just before the plebiscite, Hitler visited Vienna and described the city as "a pearl" which he was going to mount in "a worthy setting." (The Viennese often ironically quoted this remark in 1945 when the city was in ruins.) The Nazis began to draw up plans for a new "Southeastern Mission" for Austria in which Vienna was to play a key role. Much to the consternation of the Viennese and to the disillusionment of the Austrian Nazis in particular, the highest official *(Gauleiter)* in the new Reich's province of Vienna was neither Viennese nor even an Austrian Nazi but a German from Hesse, Josef Bürckel. Although the Viennese now belonged to the Reich, they resented the appointment of a German to this highest office.

Austrian Nazis, who had risked their necks for the party cause between 1933–38, expected the spoils of high positions in the Nazi administration or at least a certain amount of autonomy for the Austrian branch of the party, but these high expectations were not to be fulfilled in the least. Many Germans were imported from the Reich to fill leading positions in the Nazi administration of what had been Austria, and the Austrian branch of the party was strictly subordinated to Berlin. The Viennese viewed these facts as acts of political and cultural condescension, and they did not respond well to a tone and manner which they regarded as "Prussian": stern, humourless, pedantic, and authoritarian. The Germans, on the other hand, had a tremendous amount of difficulty adjusting to the meandering and casual Viennese way of doing things. After the initial euphoria of the *Anschluß*, the Viennese recognized that Vienna had been demoted to the status of a large but provincial city on the edge of the Reich.

In October, 1938, the Nazis created *Groß-Wien* (Greater Vienna). The city limits were revised to include 96 communities from Lower Austria which were incorporated into 5 new districts and increased the area of Vienna from 270 to 1,215 km^2. The purpose of this was to provide room for future expansion. The Nazis envisioned Vienna as a "Hamburg of the Southeast": a large trade and manufacturing centre which would utilize its proximity to the Balkans and the Danube. In the city the Nazis showed their monumentally grotesque phantasy in planning projects without ever executing them. For example, two new avenues, which were to be flanked by party buildings, were planned as extensions of the *Ringstraße*. They were to start at the points where the Ring meets the Danube Canal (*Schottenring* and *Urania*) and run straight over to the Danube. In between them, a gigantic, mock classical forum was planned for Nazi rallies. In order to realize such a plan, the Nazis would have had to destroy most of the second district, but this did not present a problem for the Nazis because most of the inhabitants in the planning area were Jews.

The German invasion of Poland on September 1, 1939, made the realization of Nazi plans for Vienna impossible because resources necessary for a large scale reconstruction of the city were allocated to the war effort. Therefore, the only lasting architectural monuments which the Nazis left in Vienna are a series of steel reinforced concrete anti-aircraft towers in the districts surrounding the Inner City. After the war, it was too complicated and expensive to tear them down, so they have survived as huge symbols of admonishment.

Persecution of the Jews

The Viennese who bore the brunt of Nazi policies and terror were the Jews. In 1938, Vienna had the second largest Jewish community in Europe (after Warsaw and ahead of Budapest), and anti-semitism had been a political tool in Vienna since the days of Lueger. The indigenous and official anti-semitism in Vienna was much worse than in other parts of the Reich, and the first few days after the *Anschluß* were accompanied by spontaneous pogroms. Many Jews were physically abused, forced to scrub streets, or clean away old Schuschnigg propaganda. Jewish stores and personal property were plundered or illegally claimed by Nazis or people pretending to be the same. The Nazi Party was interested in stopping these unauthorized actions so that Jewish property could be systematically confiscated for profit. Most of the over 185,000 Austrian Jews lived in Vienna, and they owned 33,000 (of approximately 146,000) businesses in the city ranging from small shops to factories. The official procedure of "Aryanization," a synonym for small and large scale robbery, entailed the confiscation or forced sale — under the market value — of Jewish property which was either resold for profit or put under the management of a reliable Nazi commissioner.

The systematic aryanization of Jewish property was merely a prelude to the relocation of the Jews. In August, 1938, Bürckel founded the Central Office for Jewish Emigration in Vienna, and one of its most enterprising officers was an Austrian Nazi who established an infamous reputation: Adolf Eichmann. The purpose of this office was to provide Jews with the necessary papers for emigration and to gain acess to any property, valuables, or money which had remained untouched by the aryanization process. Under Eichmann's supervision, the Central Office for Jewish Emigration worked with a speed and efficiency which became symptomatic for the "solution of the Jewish question," and after its modest beginnings in Vienna it became responsible for the registration and mass transport of Jews from all over Europe to death camps like Auschwitz.

In comparison to many European Jews, who had little or no chance of escaping the Holocaust, the Viennese Jews were relatively fortunate. Two thirds of them managed to emigrate

March, 1938; a Jewish boy being forced by a Nazi to paint Jud (Jew) on his father's store

before the war broke out, but after that the systematic deportation of Viennese Jews to the concentration camps of Eastern Europe began. In September, 1942, the Nazis declared Vienna, as the official term went, "Jew-free." Over 65,000 Austrian Jews, most of them Viennese, died in Nazi concentration camps. The few who survived were protected by mixed marriages or hidden by friends. The rapidity of the Aryanization process and relocation of Vienna's Jewish community was not merely a matter of Nazi racial theory or ideology; the apartments and houses which were vacated by emigration and deportation were redistributed by the Nazis as part of their allegedly "social" programme. This was not merely a spoils system. It was an attempt to solve the chronic Viennese housing shortage. In this manner, 70,000 flats (7,000 more than the socialist building projects had erected 1923—33) were put at the disposal of so-called Aryans.

Shifts in Attitude

The Viennese attitudes toward the *Anschluß* and National Socialism deteriorated rather rapidly once the war began, and Hitler's attempt to improve cooperation and morale by appointing a new *Gauleiter* in 1940, Baldur von Schirach, did not change the situation. The prosperity Hitler had promised in his *Heldenplatz* speech resulted in the austerity of war, and the *Heldenplatz* became a symbol for the illusion of German greatness. Like many other monuments, the two equestrian statues there were encased in brick constructions to protect them from the shrapnel of exploding bombs, and the square itself — like so many other parks throughout the city — was put into cultivation in order to provide food for the populace.

The encirclement and destruction of the German VI Army in Stalingrad during the winter of 1942—43 marked a turning point in the war on the Eastern Front as well as a watershed in the development of Austrian attitudes. From that point on, it was clear to most people that the days of Hitler's Thousand Year's Reich were numbered, and the "Germans" in Austria became increasingly more Austrian. A disproportionately large number of Austrians fought in Stalingrad, and Nazi security reports show that there was a widespread conviction among the populace that Austrians were being used as cannon fodder on the Eastern Front. The severity of the losses there is perhaps best documented by the fact that after February, 1943, normal troops were no longer used to man the *Flak* (*Flug Abwehr Kanone,* i.e. anti-aircraft cannon) positions around Vienna. Sixteen and seventeen year old boys were taken out of school for this purpose. There were over a million Austrians in German uniform during World War II, and some 250,000 of them never came home from the front.

In November, 1943, the foreign ministers of the USSR, USA, and UK, gave Austrians a remote reason for hope. At a conference in Moscow, a declaration was issued which marked the beginning of a joint Allied policy towards Austria. The Moscow Declaration stated that the Allies intended to re-establish a free and independent Austria, but it also warned that Austria did have a responsibility for participating in the war on the side of Hitler's Germany and that the Austrians' own contribution to their liberation would be taken into account after the war. This, of course, was not something the Nazis publicized, but the BBC broadcasted regularly to Austria. Although *Schwarzhören,* listening to an enemy station, was a crime severely punished, many people stayed in touch with the real course of the war in this manner.

Destruction, Resistance, and Liberation

Due to the fact that Vienna is situated so far in the East, the civilian population enjoyed a certain amount of security until late in the war because Allied bombers operating from English bases could not reach so far into the Reich. Many branches of the war industry were transferred into and around Vienna as a result. The Allied invasion of Northern Africa and Italy changed this good fortune because the Allies established air bases there which brought Central Europe into range. Wiener Neustadt, an important industrial centre 50 km south of Vienna, was bombed for the first time on August 23, 1943, and after that the Viennese prepared for the certainty of bombardment. The collection of the *Kunsthistorisches Museum,* for example, was removed and stored in empty salt mines near Salzburg for safe-keeping. A large bunker was built for the Nazi elite inside of the *Jubiläumswarte,* a large hill on the outskirts of

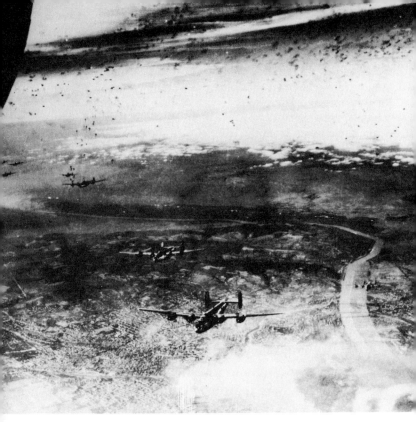

An official US Air Force photograph of bombers over Vienna during the largest Allied raid of the war on March 12, 1945; foreground: the city and the Danube; background: the black spots in the sky are exploding anti-aircraft shells

Vienna in the 16th district, but the measures for the protection of the civilian population were woefully inadequate. One of the surest signs of an approaching air raid was a procession of the limousines of the Nazi elite towards their bunker before the official alarm was sounded. The cellars of many houses were converted into makeshift air raid shelters, and occasionally the abbreviation *LSK* (*Luftschutzkeller*, i.e. air raid shelter) can be seen on the facades of old houses.

The first of 52 Allied air raids on Vienna began on March 17, 1944. After this, many mothers pilgrimed daily to the air raid shelters with their children. In spite of the imminent danger, a certain facade of normalcy was cultivated. The Vienna State Opera closed on June 30, 1944 with Wagner's *Götterdämmerung* which was an unintentionally prophetic piece of scheduling. The Opera was not re-opened after its traditional summer pause because the Nazis escalated the restrictions imposed by the declaration of "total war." Opera and theatre performances were forbidden, but concerts continued right up until the bitter end. During one performance of Brahms' *Requiem* during the Easter season, an air raid began. Refusing to be disturbed, the audience and the orchestra remained seated to continue the performance. The Vienna Philharmonic gave the "last" concert in Vienna on April 2, 1945. It was accompanied by the rumbling of artillery from the not too distant front.

The largest Allied air raid on Vienna was on March 12, 1945; a formation of 747 American bombers with a total of 1,667 tons of bombs struck the city. Although the strategic targets in Vienna were outside of the Inner City (the train stations, industrial sites in the outer districts), the historical centre of the city was hit extremeley hard. The Opera was bombed out which caused some Viennese to complain that the American pilots could not tell the difference between an opera and a train station. All of the monumental buildings on the Ring were heavily damaged, and the *Kärntnerstraße* and its adjoining streets were covered with craters. The anti-aircraft batteries actually could do very little to stop the destruction, but intense anti-aircraft fire could force attacking bombers off of a suicidal course. This was a mixed blessing because the bombers then dumped their loads on residential districts. Aside from the sheer material destruction, over 8,700 Viennese were killed in the course of Allied bombings, but Vienna and the Viennese were nevertheless relatively fortunate. The destruction and casualties in Vienna were low compared to many other cities in the Reich. Frankfurt and Dresden, for example, were practically bombed flat. The checkered pattern of old and new buildings in the Inner City, across from the Opera for example, frequently reveals exactly where the Allied bombs fell.

The austerity of the war, the news of losses on the front, and the bombings increased passive resistance in broad sections of the population which was complemented by the active resistance of small groups of individuals across the political spectrum. A Nazi situation report from March, 1945, accurately describes the atmosphere in Vienna: "Only a few still believe in the final victory . . . War weariness, irritability, and, to a certain extent, not only defeatist but also pronounced destructive tendencies can be noticed everywhere . . . This pessimistic atmosphere naturally provides a good basis for enemy propaganda. Slogans are painted on walls, flyers distributed, etc. . . . Listening to enemy radio stations is common." An example of one of the above mentioned signs of resistance can still be seen today to the right of the main entrance to St. Stephen's. A cryptonym, O5, is scratched into the facade. O plus the fifth letter of the alphabet, E, stood for *OEsterreich* and was the symbol of the Provisional Austrian National Committee, a resistance group which embraced many political convictions and attempted to coordinate efforts nationwide. The toll paid for all forms of resistance under the Nazis was high: over 16,000 Austrians died in concentration camps or Gestapo prisons, and 2,700 were executed after trials. Many of the executions took place in the *Landesgericht,* Vienna's central court house and jail which is located a few blocks behind the university.

The Battle of Vienna began in April 1945 when Soviet armies broke throught the "Southeastern Wall," a German defensive line along the Austrian-Hungarian border. On April 2, the Nazis declared Vienna a defensive zone and encouraged women and children to leave the city. The Nazis designated Vienna to be a *Festung,* a "fortress" to be held at all costs, and the city appeared to be condemned to share the fate of Budapest. Liberated after 50 days of house-to-house, block-to-block fighting in the winter of 1944–45, the "fortress" of Budapest was demolished in the process.

The brunt of the military burden of taking Vienna fell on the soldiers of the Red Army, but the activities of the Austrian resistance movement helped shorten the amount of time and number of losses necessary to free the city. On April 3, a group of Austrian officers managed to contact the headquarters of the Soviet commander and made suggestions for coordinating resistance in addition to providing tactical information and proposals. (Three of these officers were betrayed by an Austrian comrade-in-arms shortly thereafter and hanged publicly

St. Stephen's Cathedral caught fire during the Battle of Vienna in April 1945; in the foreground, Soviet soldiers

by the Nazis on the *Floridsdorfer Spitz* to set an example for the treatment of "traitors.") Soviet units broke through the defensive lines southeast of Vienna and encircled the city from the south, the west, and the north. This put the defenders of the city in an extremely precarious position. If the defensive line on the other side of the Danube did not hold, they would be surrounded on all sides with their backs to the river.

The Soviet forces tightened their noose around Vienna and drove the defenders rapidly back from the pre-1938 city limits, to the *Gürtel,* then to the Ring, across the Danube Canal, and then over the Danube. A brilliant surprise operation even enabled the Soviets to capture a major bridge over the Danube, the *Reichsbrücke,* intact. (It should have been blown up by the retreating Germans; thirty years later it collapsed for reasons unknown and has since been replaced by a modern construction.) Artillery duels increased the amount of damage throughout the city, and as the German defenders withdrew they took, regardless of the obvious consequences, all of the Vienna Fire Department's equipment with them. In the course of Soviet-German artillery duels, a number of fires broke out throughout the city. The most tragic and spectacular was at St. Stephen's Cathedral. The cathedral had miraculously survived Allied bombings and the artillery duels, but on April 10, a fire from a neighbouring building carried over to the cathedral's damaged roof, burned for three days, and left the cathedral a charred shell. Some Viennese civilians desparately attempted to squelch the flames with a bucket brigade, but their efforts were as hopeless as they were heroic.

Most of the Viennese did not directly experience the Battle of Vienna which cost over 37,000 Soviet and German soldiers their lives. Locking the doors to their houses to keep the soldiers and the fighting out in the streets, they retreated to the cramped confines of their cellars. They could hear the sounds of battle outside but really did not know what was happening out on the street or in the next block. After the front swept through any given neighbourhood, Soviet military commandos systematically searched every house for soldiers and weapons, and they found many Viennese in the process. This was the first contact the Viennese had with the soldiers of the Red Army, and their response was mixed and ambivalent. Some Viennese viewed them as enemies, others at first saw them as liberators, many people were really not sure what they should think or expect, but almost everyone feared the victorious troops. The uncertainty of war ended, and the uncertainty of peace began.

X. The Aftermath: Allied Occupation

While the Battle of Vienna was still raging, Austrian politicians emerged from the underground. As soon as the Nazis had been driven across the Danube, members of the Provisional Austrian National Committee (O5) began meeting in *Palais Auersperg* to discuss Austria's future. Independently the political parties re-established themselves in buildings symbolic of their traditions. The Socialist Party of Austria *(Sozialistische Partei Österreichs, SPÖ)* was constituted in the *Rathaus* and assumed the tradition of the First Republic's Social Democrats. The Austrian People's Party *(Österreichische Volkspartei, ÖVP)* was founded in the *Schottenstift,* the Benedictine monastery on the *Freyung,* and re-assumed the traditional conservative values of the Christian Social movement. Both political camps had undergone ideological transformations during the Nazi occupation. The socialists abandoned the Marxist jargon which had threatened the middle class and rural populace, and the conservatives renounced those parts of their political tradition which were authoritarian and anti-democratic.

Many politicians, who had so bitterly opposed each other before 1938, met as common enemies of National Socialism in the concentration camps and prisons of the Third Reich. Having developed close friendships which were cemented by their common desire to see Austria re-established, they realized that the only way to master the problems of Allied occupation and reconstruction was to demonstrate cooperation, unity, and tolerance. The ideological hatchets of the past were buried, for the time being at least, and one of the results was more than two decades of coalition governments in which the major parties shared responsibilities and power. The newly formed parties also had to reckon with the Communist Party of Austria *(KPÖ)* which was an opponent of unknown strength whose leaders had returned from Soviet exile in the wake of the Red Army.

From Chaos to Order

One Communist made his presence felt immediately although his activities were not sanctioned by the KPÖ. After the Nazis had been driven across the Danube, an obscure figure, Josef Prykril, assumed the position of "commissary mayor" in the *Rathaus*. Self-appointed and armed with a rubber stamp, which had the communist hammer and sickle next to his title, he single-handedly began administering the city. He officially assigned apartments, made appointments, wrote certifications, and confiscated the property of Nazis who had fled. His unusual period in office was facilitated by two factors: the situation in Vienna was chaotic, and the Viennese as well as the Soviet soldiers demonstrated a deeply ingrained respect for bureaucracy. Prykril's rubber stamp was a clear sign of authority and gave the impression of creating order out of chaos.

The self-proclaimed mayor's brief period in office was ended by the representatives of the three "democratic and anti-fascist" parties, the SPÖ, ÖVP, and KPÖ, whose representatives agreed upon the socialist Theodor Körner, a retired general from the Imperial Army and former *Schutzbund* commander, as a provisional mayor until the next free elections could be held. This recommendation was approved by the Soviet commander of Vienna, and municipal government re-assumed its activities on April 19 after the *Rathaus* had been routinely searched for weapons. The political situation in Vienna was certainly peculiar. Political parties came back into being before an Austrian state existed, and they agreed upon a candidate for provisional mayor who, for the time being, represented the only recognized Austrian civil authority. During all of this, the Germans still occupied the part of Vienna across the Danube. The Soviets did not take *Floridsdorf* until April 22.

While Viennese politicians were busy re-establishing municipal government, Dr. Karl Renner, one of the First Republic's most eminent socialist politicians, emerged from retirement to begin a second political career. The 74 year old Renner lived in Gloggnitz about 75 km southwest of Vienna and had encouraged the local population not to flee from the Red Army. Some civilians were mistreated by Soviet troops, and the people complained to Renner who immediately took his walking stick and left home without a coat to complain to the local commander. The Soviets recognized his stature and importance immediately and passed him up the chain of command. To a certain extent, the establishment of the Second Republic began with the walk and complaints Renner initially intended to make. Shortly thereafter, he entered onto high level negotiations with the Soviets which, unusually enough, were initially independent of any contacts the Soviets had with the newly founded parties in Vienna.

On April 27, 1945, nine days after the appointment of Körner as provisional mayor, the political parties proclaimed Austrian independence and a provisional government was formed under Renner's leadership. The position of Renner's government was a unique as it was precarious. The war had not ended, only a small part of Eastern Austria had been liberated, and the remainder was still under German control. As an act of political circumspection and a demonstration of democratic principles, Renner had also included two Communists in the provisional cabinet. This raised the suspicions of the Western Allies and many Western Austrians who did not participate in the formation of the government and suspected that it was a communist puppet. In spite of all these difficulties, Austria was re-established, and Vienna was an Austrian city once again.

Vienna's cultural life also quickly came back to life. The first postwar concert was held on April 27. Clemens Krauss conducted the Philharmonic with a programme of Beethoven, Schubert, and Tschaikowsky. After seven years of Nazi cultural censorship, it was the first time Tschaikowskij could be performed. The *Burgtheater* and the State Opera were bombed out, but their ensembles reorganized to perform in the *Ronacher Theater* and the *Volksoper*. The *Burg* opened on April 30 with a production of Grillparzer, and the State Opera's company performed *The Marriage of Figaro* on May Day. Shortly thereafter, the State Opera moved to the *Theater an der Wien*, a small house where Beethoven had conducted the first performance of *Fidelio* and which now specializes in musicals ranging from *Jesus Christ Superstar* to *Cats*. This temporary solution lasted for over a decade. The flurry of cultural activity was not merely a spontaneous outburst of Viennese dedication to the arts; the Soviets were in a cultural metropolis and demanded performances. The Viennese wanted and had to resume cultural activities.

Adolf Hitler committed suicide in his Berlin bunker on April 30, the war in Europe ended on May 8, 1945, and Vienna was left with the following balance: over 20% of the city's residential buildings were destroyed or damaged to an extent which made them uninhabitable; most bridges throughout the city had been destroyed; the streets were full of bomb craters; sewage, water, and gas lines were broken; there was no electricity and rubble everywhere. Medical services had broken down completely, and civilian and military dead were buried in parks and yards if at all. The supply of food for the civilian population collapsed completely.

The war was over, but numerous Soviet soldiers conducted themselves in a manner which confirmed the worst prophecies of Nazi propaganda: raping, plundering, and looting. The acts of large and small scale robbery were by no means confined to Soviet troops; some of the Viennese took the opportunity to help themselves too. In light of the initial conduct of some of the Soviet troops, the Viennese responded with a morbid and ironical observation: "We could survive another war, . . . but not another liberation." The only immediate aid the Soviets could provide given the situation was dried peas and beans which had to be sorted one-by-one for worms.

Some older Viennese, who experienced the end of the Second World War, often refer to it with a broad but encompassing term, *der Zusammenbruch* or collapse. Seldom does anyone refer to it as the *Befreiung* or liberation. What had collapsed was Hitler's 1000 Years' Reich, and amidst the rubble, the Viennese were not sure what was to follow. An attitude of uncertainty and desperation was slowly replaced by cautious optimism and hope. In 1918, the collapse of the Austro-Hungarian monarchy had left Vienna intact but demoralized. In 1945, the collapse of the German Reich left Vienna in shambles. However, after the initial confusion passed, a spirit of national and moral rejuvenation seized the younger generation in particular. Reconstruction was a mission.

The experience of Nazi rule and the war had effectively "denazified" most Austrians, but after the war official legislation was implemented. Nazi party members were expelled from

A post-war Viennese street scene; civilians crossing the rubble of houses destroyed by bombing and battle

public service, lost pensions, apartments, and small plots of land, *Schrebergärten*. Subjected to highly graduated taxes, they were also forced to remove rubble from the streets or exhume hastily buried corpses, and, in some cases, put on trial and imprisoned. Ironically, many party members were either no longer convinced Nazis or never had been in the first place.

Many people had joined the party as opportunists or were required to do so as a mere matter of survival. All of these "Nazis" were thrown into one category, and, in some cases, the prosecution and amnesty policies were inconsistent. Today, some small and isolated right wing groups continue to flirt with the Nazi past. Walking the fine line between what they call "nationalism" and the illegal propagation of neo-Nazi ideas, these die-hards seek new recruits among the young and the discontented.

Occupation and Four Power Control

The Allied agreements dealing with the occupation and administration of Austria were signed in the course of the summer of 1945. Austria, in spite of its federal government, was divided into four little Austrias and one Vienna which, in turn, was divided into four little Viennas with the 1ˢᵗ district as an international zone. The French occupied Vorarlberg and Tyrol; the British, East Tyrol, Carinthia, and Styria; the Americans, Salzburg and the portion of Upper Austria south of the Danube; and the Russians, Upper Austria north of the Danube, Lower Austria, and Burgenland. Within each of these zones, the respective Allied commander exercised his powers autonomously. Vienna was divided in a similar manner. The French occupied four districts in the western part of the city (6, 14, 15, 16); the Americans six districts in the central and northwestern parts (7, 8, 9, 17, 18, 19); the Soviets three districts east of the Danube Canal (2, 20, 21) and two districts in the south (4, 10); and the British the remaining 5 districts in the south and southwestern corners of the city (3, 5, 11, 12, 13). The 1ˢᵗ district was an international sector which was administered on a rotating monthly basis by each of the Allies.

Four power bodies were established for the joint administration of Austria (the Allied Council) and Vienna (the Inter-Allied Command). By the beginning of September 1945, these organs began functioning and Western occupational contingents had been transferred to Vienna. The Allied commanders held their first official meeting in the Soviet occupied Hotel Imperial. The women of Vienna responded to the presence of the Western occupational forces with their own feminine sign of confidence. They stopped wearing scarfs and started wearing hats.

The situation of Vienna was a microcosm of Allied-Austrian relations. The provisional government was finally recognized by the Allies on October 20, 1945 — over six months after it had been established — and Austria's first free and democratic national elections since 1930 were held on November 25. Against all expectations and fears, the communists did very poorly by polling only 5% of the votes. A disappointment to the Soviets and a relief for the Western Allies as well as the SPÖ

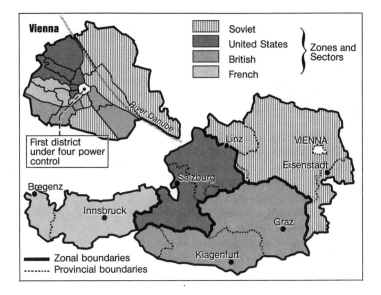

Vienna

Soviet
United States
British
French

Zones and
Sectors

River Danube

First district
under four power
control

Linz

VIENNA

Eisenstadt

Bregenz

Salzburg

Innsbruck

Graz

Klagenfurt

Zonal boundaries
Provincial boundaries

and ÖVP, the KPÖ was not to play a decisive role in Austrian politics. Even though the Austrian Federal Parliament resumed its activity in December 1945, the Allied Council acted as a higher political instance which reserved the power to block, amend, and send back legislation to the Austrian Parliament. A similar relationship existed between the city of Vienna and the Inter-Allied Command. In addition to these joint Allied bodies on a national and municipal level, the individual zonal commanders in the provinces and in Vienna could exercise their powers practically at random. They were a supra-legal instance which neither local nor federal authorities could control. At first, controls were set up at all zonal borders, and an Allied ID card issued in four languages was an absolute necessity for everyone. The controls among the Western sectors were loosened rather quickly but rigorously executed by the Soviets who used them to interfere with the passage of persons and goods entering or leaving Vienna.

The treatment of the civilian population as well as the freedom with which Austrian government officials were allowed to perform their duties differed from zone to zone, from East to West in particular. Some Austrian officials were accused of

A symbol of Allied occupation and cooperation: "four in a jeep"

anti-Soviet espionage, arrested in the Russian zone, and imprisoned. Each of the occupying powers followed a different policy, and, among other things, established their own newspapers. The *Kurier,* one of Austria's most popular dailies, was
originally printed by the American occupational forces in
Vienna.

Although the relationship between the Soviet Union and
the Western Allies became increasingly strained in the immediate post-war period, there was one sign of cooperation in
Vienna which survived all of the tensions of the Cold War, "the
four in a jeep." Vienna had a unique international military
patrol. Representatives from each of the four powers were
assigned to common duty in one jeep, and these Inter-Allied
patrols could operate all over the city. The "four in a jeep" were
not only a practically isolated example of cooperation during
the deepest chill of the Cold War but also a microcosm which
reflected political and ideological tensions. If the four in a jeep
were a symbol for the occupation of Vienna, four elephants in a
rowboat became the symbol for the occupation of Austria. The
burden of occupation was excruciatingly heavy.

Liberated but not Free

The situation of the Viennese in the immediate post-war years was extremely dire. Food was rationed, but the irregularity of supply often made the ration cards worthless. There was a lack of heating materials and medicine. Infant mortality rose to 18%, the undernourishment of children and adults alike was common, and the Vienna Woods once again became a source of fuel. Soup lines were set up at many schools for children under twelve, but the lack of meat forced improvisation. The Americans, for example, often served a soup made of powdered milk and raisins. In addition to Allied aid, many public and church organizations throughout Western Europe organ-

A soup line for children organized by the Allies after the war

ized relief programmes in Austria. Foster homes were offered to Viennese children, and child transports left Vienna regularly by rail. The children were addressed like packages. A small card was hung around their necks with their names and destinations and a return address in Vienna. After months, or in some cases over a year abroad, some parents did not recognize their children when they went to pick them up at the train station because they had gained so much weight. Until years after the war, bananas and oranges were unknown to most children who tried to eat these fruits with the peels on the first time they had them.

The shortage of virtually everything led to widerspread black marketeering. The *Naschmarkt* and the *Resselpark* near *Karlsplatz* were illicit centres of trade. Both the German and then the reformed Austrian currency were absolutely worthless on the black market where the primary currency during 1945–46 was cigarettes and cigarette lighter flints; one flint was equal to six cigarettes. To a certain extent, the Allied clients in each of the occupational zones protected their black marketeers in order to guarantee an uninterrupted supply of merchandise. Austrian officials were helpless because they could not control the passage of materials on Allied vehicles. The Viennese police in the Soviet occupied districts could not arrest persons in Russian uniform, even if they were caught committing a crime, nor could the police use their weapons against such individuals, not even in self-defense. As a result, many of the black marketeers and criminals acquired Russian uniforms and the immunity which went with them. Those who had nothing to trade or barter often brought themselves to the marketplace. It was common to see young teenage girls waiting outside of the Allied barracks prepared to trade sexual favours for chocolate. Black marketeering, espionage, and corruption became a disreputable Viennese cliché after Carol Reed filmed Graham Greene's novel, *The Third Man.* Orson Welles, cast as the shadowy Harry Lime, and his even shadowier Viennese counterparts, played by leading members of the *Burgtheater* ensemble, were just as much a part of Viennese reality as they were a product of literary or cinematic imagination.

Reconstruction

In 1947, the European Recovery Programme, better known as the Marshall Plan, marked the beginning of the end of the black market. A clear East-West economic watershed developed in Austria. In 1946, the Soviets claimed the so-called "German assets" in their occupational zones. According to Allied agreements, the Soviets were entitled to the German assets in their zones of occupation throughout Eastern Europe, but distinguishing between pre-1938 Austrian assets and the German investment and properties which had been accumulated from 1938 until 1945 was no simple matter. The Soviets chose a simple form of interpretation which best corresponded to their immediate needs and claimed approximately half of Austria's industrial potential. A special Soviet organization, USIA, was set up to administer the German assets in eastern Austria, and it systematically exploited Austrian natural and industrial resources without paying taxes or delivering goods to the Austrian market. To protect the economy, the Austrian Parliament nationalized major banks and industries. This was hardly a matter of socialist management. The USIA represented a tremendous burden on Austria which was counterbalanced by over a billion dollars of Marshall Plan aid.

Reconstruction in Vienna progressed slowly at first and accelerated as the Austrian economy began to stabilize. The holes torn into the city by the war were slowly filled, and Vienna began a second phase of municipal building. The city administration was forced to build quickly and cheaply and was not always able to maintain the social and architectural standards which had guided the golden age of municipal building during the interwar period. The urgency of the housing problem is a partial explanation for the plain ugliness of municipal (as well as private) building done at that time, but it is by no means an excuse for the lack of ingenuity often shown since then. Many houses in the 50's were built in a style which was ironically labeled "Swiss cheese." They were blocks with holes.

The first phase of the reconstruction of St. Stephen's Cathedral ended in 1948 when the nave was completed. Reopened for worship at that time, it took another four years to repair the damage done to the choir. A traditional symbol of

Vienna, St. Stephen's became a symbol for the Republic of Austria in the course of its reconstruction. Each of the provinces contributed to the worthy cause, and a simple plaque in the nave not only records the extent of the damage which had been done but also documents the collective national effort: "The bell which calls you into this house of God was donated by Upper Austria; the portal which opens the cathedral to you, by Styria; the stone floor which carries your steps, by Lower Austria; the pews in which you kneel to pray, by Vorarlberg; the windows which let in the light of the heavens, by Tyrol; the candleholders which shine in festive light, by Carinthia; the communion rail where you receive the body of the Lord, by Burgenland; the tabernacle in front of which your soul bows in respect, by Salzburg; the roof, which protects the holiest place in this province, by the Municipality of Vienna in union with many helping hands."

The hopes reconstruction awoke were often overshadowed by Austria's uncertain political future. The negotiation of the Austrian State Treaty began in 1947, but broke down completely in 1950 as East-West relations deteriorated in the course of the Cold War. The Western Austrians were much more exuberant and confident than the Viennese who had always tolerated political oppression with a combination of deferential charm and oblique resistance. Austria was used as a pawn in the East-West conflict. Each report of yet another meeting raised hopes which were inevitably shattered by a report of no progress. A film made at that time best described the irony of the Viennese. *1. April 2000* was a satire on what everyday life in Vienna would be like after well over fifty years of occupation.

Towards Freedom and Neutrality

Although the Iron Curtain ran through Austria and Vienna, it would have been difficult for the occupying powers to divide them like Germany and Berlin. In comparison to Germany, the Allies were committed to the re-establishment of Austria, and the Austrian federal government was recognized by all of the

occupational powers. The Allied Council continued to function in spite of the Cold War, and neither the Soviets nor the
Austrian Communists enjoyed popular support. In contrast to
Berlin, Vienna had an international sector in the 1st district, and
the British zone of occupation split the Russian zone in two.

The death of Stalin in 1953, combined with the brief thaw in
East-West relations which followed, provided an unexpected
opportunity for renewing the negotiation of the State Treaty.
One of the biggest problems dealt with the future military status
of Austria. The Americans found the idea of having Russian
troops in Vorarlberg and Tyrol just as intolerable as the Russians found the possibility of NATO troops in Eastern Austria.
After all, Vienna is further East than Prague or Berlin. It
became apparent to Austrian politicians that non-alignment
would be the only status acceptable to both sides, and they
began discussing the possibility of a neutrality similar to that of
Switzerland for Austria . . . first among themselves and then
informally with representatives of the occupational forces. The
idea of Austrian neutrality broke the diplomatic stalemate surrounding the State Treaty. Neither the East nor the West had
anything to gain or to lose through the re-establishment of
Austrian sovereignty because a neutral state is obliged to avoid
any military commitments which surpass defending its own
borders. On the one hand, Austria's declaration of neutrality
was voluntary, but, on the other, it was the precondition for the
superpowers' signatures on the State Treaty.

During April and May, 1955, Austrian diplomats managed
to resolve the open bilateral questions with the East and the
West, and the foreign ministers of the signatory powers signed
the Austrian State Treaty in the Belvedere Palace on May 15,
1955. A large crowd of Viennese spontaneously collected in
the park of the palace and anxiously waited for some sign of
finality. Suddenly the Austrian Foreign Minister Leopold Figl
appeared on the balcony of the palace with the foreign ministers of the signatory powers. With tears in his eyes, he held up
the freshly signed treaty and said: *Österreich ist frei!* The Viennese were relieved and joyous.

The State Treaty ended the occupation of Austria. It was
ratified by the signatory powers in the course of the summer,
the last Allied troops left Vienna on October 14, 1955, and by

October 25, all of the occupational forces had withdrawn from Austrian territory. On October 26, the first day Austrian territorial sovereignty was fully re-established, the Austrian Parliament unanimously and voluntarily passed a constitutional amendment establishing Austria's permanent neutrality. (Neutrality, as important as it was in the negotiation of the State Treaty, is not legally anchored there or even mentioned in the text. This would have given the signatory powers the right to interpret Austrian neutrality. Austria's unilateral and constitutional declaration of neutrality avoided that problem by making neutrality a principle of foreign policy.)

Permanent neutrality marked not only a redefinition of Austria's international status but also the beginning of a new role for the city of Vienna. Until 1955, Vienna was an outpost in the Cold War, the easternmost foxhole of the West in the East; after 1955, Vienna was at worst neutral ground and at best a meeting place for the East and the West. Austria was free, and on November 5, 1955, the reconstructed State Opera opened with Beethoven's *Fidelio,* the story of an unjustly held captive.

XI. Old Problems and
New Impulses

The ten years of Allied occupation were by no means an optimal basis for reconstruction, but they nevertheless were the beginning of Austria's post-war success story. The trials of National Socialism and the tribulations of Allied occupation instilled the Austrians with a cooperative spirit. The ÖVP—SPÖ coalition goverments lasted on a national level until 1966, and in Vienna, where the spirit of confrontation had formerly been strongest, the coalition between the socialists and the conservatives in the *Rathaus* endured until 1973. Cooperation, hard work, and Western aid provided a sound foundation for the Austrian economy, and there was a fluid transition from the reconstruction of the 50's to the prosperity of the 60's and thereafter.

In the process, Austria also developed a unique and internationally acknowledged method of resolving the traditional conflicts between labour and management as well as industry and agriculture. Leading representatives of these different economic interest groups meet regularly to discuss questions of common concern, like wages and prices, and work out collective solutions to the problems before they reach the critical point of confrontation. This peculiarly Austrian practice called *Sozialpartnerschaft* (Social Partnership) is not anchored in the constitution or in legislation but in common sense and goodwill. If one of the weak points of the First Republic was an inability to resolve problems politically, then one of the Second Republic's keys to success has been the ability to solve many problems of common concern with as little politics as possible. Social Partnership has contributed greatly to the political and economic stability of Austria. For example, the amount of labour time lost by strikes in Austria is not measured annually per capita in hours, days, or weeks, but in minutes.

Neutrality demands a balanced foreign policy which fundamentally involves maintaining the confidence of the West and not arousing the suspicions of the East. Austria shares borders with Warsaw Pact and COMECON members, Czechoslovakia and Hungary, NATO and Common Market members, Italy and the Federal Republic of Germany, communist but non-aligned Yugoslavia, and neutral Switzerland. Relationships with immediate neighbours as well as the superpowers have been carefully cultivated. Austria's circumspective practice of neutrality has helped Vienna reassume its old historical role as a crossroads in the heart of Europe.

Neutrality has also made Austria a haven of asylum for refugees from all over the world and the former lands of the Habsburg Empire in the East in particular. After the Hungarian Revolution in 1956, before the Soviet invasion of Czechoslovakia ended the Prague Spring in 1968, and during the crises surrounding the Solidarity movement in Poland in the early 80's, tens of thousands of people fled their communist homes and sought asylum in neutral Austria. Most of them moved on to new homes throughout the world, but for some temporary asylum became permanent residency. This has enriched Vienna's old multinational tradition in a particularly modern manner.

The Limitations of Innovation

Vienna and the Viennese endured the calamities of the first half of the 20th century and recovered to prosper. After World War II, Vienna continued to administer some areas of Lower Austria on the city's borders. In 1954 two new districts were incorporated and added to the city's previous twenty one. The modern large scale industrial and residential development of the city has since been concentrated on the eastern and southern peripheries of Vienna where a series of satellite projects have been developed. Expansion was only one of the challenges the city planners faced; another was to deal with urban structures which were a product of the 19th century and in some cases hopelessly outdated. Vienna has been confronted with problems of the past, and the solutions of the present have to be tailored to meet the demands of preserving the city's historical heritage.

Modernization has therefore consistently been tempered by a spirit of conservation in Vienna, and one of the municipal administration's mottos has been "plan modern but keep the charm." Even though there have been occasional lapses in the past, the old has not been indiscriminately torn down to be replaced by the new. On the contrary, it is carefully renovated and adapted to meet modern needs. The restoration and renovation of historical buildings — not only monuments like churches and palaces but also apartment houses, old public transporation stations, and, in some cases, 19th century factories — are high priorities. Building codes are strictly enforced, and, as a result, Vienna has maintained its old appearance. Vienna is one of the few cities in the world where new buildings are sometimes required to look old. Recently an office building was erected on *Schwarzenberg-Platz,* and the city required the contractors to give it a *Ringstraße*facade so that it would fit into its immediate historical surroundings.

The infamous legacy of 19th century residential housing can still be felt today even though the population shift out of the older central districts to the periphery has alleviated the problem to a certain extent. Almost half of Vienna's residential buildings were built before World War I. Approximately 25% of Vienna's apartments are under 45 m^2 — 1 to 2 rooms — and almost 50% are under 60 m^2. In 1970, 20% of Vienna's flats had no running water and 33.5% had no toilet inside. By 1980, these figures were reduced by approximately half, but there are still over 100,000 flats in Vienna without one or the other of these common conveniences. The *Bassena* has survived, and less than 50% of Viennese households have central heating, a bathroom, and a toilet. The municipality has done its best to alleviate these circumstances, and makeshift solutions are particularly common in small flats where a bathtub or a shower stall can frequently be found in the kitchen. Vienna subsidizes improvements, if renters are willing to invest, by providing interest free loans, and progress is being made.

The relatively low standard of Viennese housing has always made recreational areas and facilities outside of the home and the city important. The Vienna Woods are still a favourite place

169

for a walk on Sunday afternoon, and a new attraction, the *Donau Insel,* has recently been completed. This 20 km long and 200 meter wide island in the Danube was designed as part of a flood control project, but it doubles as a recreational area for bicyclists, fishermen, sailors, windsurfers, and sunbathers. On nice weekends, tens of thousands of people storm the island which is promoted as the Adriatic — a traditional destination for vacationing Viennese — on the Danube. For the less active, there is still the coffee-house which has been classically defined as a place where one is "not at home but nevertheless not in the fresh air." The Viennese counterparts of the pub and the inn, the *Beisl* and the *Gasthaus,* are flourishing, a frequent meeting place for friends from the neighbourhood, and have been called the Viennese alternative to the living room as a result. The popularity of the *Heurigen,* the coffee-house, the wine keller, the *Gasthaus* is partially related to the cramped quarters and low standard of Viennese housing. The fortunate also have some place to go outside of the city. The modest aspire to a *Schrebergarten*: a small plot of land with a hut, a fruit tree or two, and a few flowers or vegetables which are religiously cultivated. Entire communities of *Schrebergärten* can be found in and around Vienna. The wealthier Viennese aspire to a weekend house in the country, and these second residences are sprinkled all over Lower Austria and Burgenland.

Vienna has also continued the tradition of communal building, owns over 210,000 living units today, and is landlord for almost a quarter of the city's households. Nevertheless, the era of communal housing appears to be drawing to a close. On the one hand, building costs — and therefore rents — for municipal apartments have risen tremendously, and, on the other, these apartments are still in principle assigned according to the criteria of social need. Due to the high rents, many low income families cannot afford to move into them. There are also isolated cases of families in modern, expensive communal housing who simply cannot afford the rent on their low incomes. As a result, the city is put in a paradoxical position where the spirit of communal housing and the demands of modern financing collide head on. Can the Municipality of Vienna dislodge a tenant for not paying rent when the family was assigned a municipal apartment upon the basis of social need in the first place?

Traditional Structures

In spite of the recent development of the city, many of the old social structures of Vienna still exist. A survey of the city based on the criteria of housing quality (apartment size and modern conveniences) and the educational level of residents (mandatory, secondary, and higher education), both of which are indicative of different income groups, allows the following generalizations. The districts 3—9 which immediately surround the Inner City are still fundamentally middle class in character, and the traditional working class districts (2, 10—12, 15—17, 20, 21) have predominantly lower income groups and frequently substandard housing. The "noble" districts near *Schönbrunn* (13, 14) or near *Grinzing* and the Vienna Woods (18, 19) are more or less upper class and well-to-do. The new satellite projects (on the outskirts of 10 and 11, in 21, 22, and the eastern part of 23) represent a qualitatively high standard of housing, which is inhabited by lower income groups, whereas the recent development of areas on the outskirts of the districts bordering the Vienna Woods in the western parts of the city is predominantly upper class in character.

The population shift out of the city to the periphery, from substandard to modern housing, and from asphalt and cement to grass and trees is indicative of a demographic pattern also. The population of Vienna has dropped steadily from its World War I peak of 2.2 million to less than 1.6 today. The older neighbourhoods inside and bordering the *Gürtel* have an unusually high percentage of elder residents. Younger ones often try to move out to the periphery of the city which has created a demographic imbalance in many districts. There are approximately 700,000 registered housholds in Vienna, and 260,000 Viennese live alone. The retired account for 318,000 Viennese households — over 40% — and more than half of these senior citizens live alone. The Viennese have a great affection for pets, but old age and loneliness apparently also contribute to the city's large canine population. There are over 60,000 dogs in the city.

Compared to other major European cities, Vienna has a high mean age which indicates a disproportionately large number of senior citizens, a low birth rate, and small average family size. The predominance of the older generation is one explanation for the traditionalism of the Viennese, but it would be inaccurate to reduce the Viennese sense of tradition to this denominator. The prevailing interest in conserving things of the past is not just the natural inflexibility of older generations; it is a matter of conviction which has been passed onto the young with varying degrees of success.

The economic upswing of the 60's and the clever economic management of the 70's provided most Viennese with an unprecedented, if modest, amount of material prosperity. This has narrowed the traditional material gap between the higher and lower classes without really changing the social structures or the political alignments of the city. The mayor and the City Council have been socialist since World War II. In spite of the nationalization of Austria's key industries after the war, Vienna has maintained an almost Biedermeier economic structure. In the age of multinationals, over 90% of Vienna's businesses have less than 20 employees and over half of those less than five. The chain store and the supermarket are competing with the family owned shop and the local grocer, but many Viennese still prefer the familiarity of the personal touch to the sterile efficiency of the chain store. Politicians and citizens are mutually concerned about the preservation of the traditional suppliers of consumer goods. If the local butcher, baker, and grocer close down, the quality of life in a given neighbourhood drops, for the elderly in particular who are not so mobile. Local merchants interpreted the opening of an American-style shopping centre south of Vienna in 1980 as a bad omen of things to come.

If Vienna was a city of bureaucrats, servants, and wage earners in the 19th century, it has become a city of white collar workers — and bureaucrats — in the 20th. Well over half of the city's labour force is engaged in service industries. The security of a permanent job is highly valued, and very few people have the capital or necessary inclination to take the risks involved in self-employment. Only 50,000 Viennese are self-employed; 730,000 are employees. Careers are not made by moving around and changing jobs. Patient service and connections within one organization or company are generally recognized and accepted as the way of gradually making it to the top. Careers are not steep and exciting but a matter of gradual promotion and endurance. Many wives and mothers work, not as an expression of emancipation but because one-and-a-half incomes are a simple matter of necessity for most families. The traditional Viennese modesty and ability to enjoy simple pleasures is partially economically inspired. There are many families who lost everything once during the post-World War I inflation, a second time during the Great Depression, and a third time at the end of World War II. The older generation has attempted to pass on the virtues of thrift and modesty to the younger generation which has grown up relatively prosperous.

Internationalization

Austria's geographical position between East and West and political status as a neutral state have made Vienna an increasingly important international centre in the past decades. The Soviet Union and the United States have held important summit meetings in Vienna. John F. Kennedy and Nikita Khrushchev conferred in Schönbrunn Palace in June, 1961, and Jimmy Carter and Leonid Breshnev signed the Strategic Arms Limitations Talks II Agreement in Vienna in 1979. The treaty was not ratified by the US Congress, but at the time Austrian Federal Chancellor Bruno Kreisky optimistically drew a local historical parallel by comparing the importance of SALT II for European peace and security in the 20th century to that of the Vienna Congress in the 19th. Aside from these diplomatic spectacles, Vienna has contributed to the East-West dialogue by hosting the MBFR Talks, which are aimed at a reduction of conventional forces in Europe, since 1974, but the representatives from NATO and the Warsaw Pact have made very little progress.

Vienna not only provides a neutral ground for the resolution of differences between the superpowers. It is an optimal setting for the work of international organizations. The International Atomic Energy Agency moved their permanent seat to Vienna in 1957 and was followed by the United Nations Industrial Development Organization in 1967 which made Vienna — after New York and Geneva — the world's third "UN

Kennedy, Austrian Federal President Schärf, and Khrushchev (l. to r.) during an East-West summit in Vienna; June, 1961

city." The Austrian federal government and the Municipality of Vienna subsidized the construction of an 8.8 billion schilling complex near the Danube for the UN. The Vienna International Centre (VIC) now houses over 3,000 UN employees from all over the world and is leased to the United Nations by Austria for a nominal rent of one schilling per year. The completion of the VIC in 1979 resulted in the transfer of a number of smaller UN agencies from New York to Vienna, and, in some cases, the UN officials involved were not exactly enthusiastic about their new home. Vienna does not possess the raw vitality and excitement of Manhattan, and some diplomats, who have been stationed in New York, Paris or Tokyo, find the city provincial. Others develop a completely different life-style that involves adjusting to Viennese rhythms and rituals.

Vienna has also attracted a number of other international organizations. OPEC has its central office in Vienna, and many of the worlds leading multinationals are also represented in the city. A sincere effort has been made to make all of these guests feel at home. A mosque has been recently constructed north of the VIC to provide the Muslims of the international community with a place of worship. The cross and the crescent moon of Islam — symbols of previous conflicts — now peacefully co-exist on the Danube. Vienna hosts a large international community without really integrating them into the city. The average Viennese regards the important and sometimes exotic members of the international community with a combination of reservation and respect. The transience and the cohesiveness of the international community combined with the reclusive privacy many Viennese still cultivate make cross-cultural contacts difficult for guests and hosts alike.

The internationalization of Vienna has not just occured on the highest social and diplomatic levels. The international community of UN officials, diplomats, and executives, who pre-

Two modern symbols of Vienna: the "UNO City" (Vienna International Centre) and the U-Bahn

dominantly live in the traditional noble districts (13, 14, 18, 19) represent only a minority of the foreigners in the city. The great majority are *Gastarbeiter* (guest workers) who were attracted to Austria during the economic boom years and provided direly needed labour power. Although few (3.3%) of these foreign workers have the intention of making Austria their permanent home, they have become a permanent feature of the economy and provide a large reservoir of unskilled labour for manual and menial tasks. Approximately 70% of Austria's guest workers — 50,000 Yugoslavs and 25,000 Turks — are concentrated in Vienna, and they most frequently live in districts with a high percentage of substandard housing. The city's oldest working class neighbourhood, the 16th district, *Ottakring,* hosts the largest number of foreign workers. The size of this foreign community — and the presence of the Turks in particular — has led to the ironical remark that the Turks have finally won the siege of Vienna after 300 years.

Like the international community, the guest workers, who are on the absolutely lowest rung of the social ladder, do not have much personal contact with the Viennese. Most residents view the strange ways of these less prestigious guests with a certain uneasiness and ill-founded distrust, and exaggerated prejudices are frequently reinforced by guest workers' own lack of interest in short-term assimilation. The children of guest workers suffer because they grow up in between two cultures. They are neither Viennese nor do they feel at home in their parents' country of origin. Some conscientious municipal and private initiatives have been taken to help integrate the members of Vienna's international community — from both ends of the social spectrum — into the life of the city. They have not been overnight successes, but they do represent an important start.

The University of Vienna, the Academy of Music and Performing Arts, and the Vienna Conservatory have also brought a tremendous number of foreign students to the city. A student from the Far East with a violin case in hand or an Arab or African in the University library are commonplace, and a fair number of Western European and American students have been attracted to Vienna, too. The medieval international tradition of the *Alma Mater Rudolphina* has assumed new and global dimensions.

Tourists also contribute to the international flair of Vienna. At the peak of the seasonal flood of travellers, more English, not to mention French, Italian, or Japanese, is heard on the *Kärntnerstraße* than German. Almost a million tourists frequent Vienna each year to see the sights and catch a whiff of the old Imperial atmosphere which can still be found in the city. Tourism is one of Vienna's most important industries, and it contributes in its own way to the preservation of the city. Most tourists come to consume Vienna's past, not experience its present; however, the tourist industry has also indirectly contributed to the destruction of some old Viennese instutions and habits. As soon as something as indigenous as tradition is reproduced, packaged, and marketed for foreign consumption, it has a tendency to wither and die. In spite of this, the genuine somehow manages to survive side-by-side with the artificial. Around the corner from the over-priced, fake 18th century *Heurigen,* which was designed to absorb 6 busloads of tourists, the real thing can still be found.

Traditionalisms

A high degree of differentiation has always existed in Viennese society. Fundamentally determined by an individual's family background, there have been and are generally recognized and accepted distinctions between social groups. These distinctions were formerly based on real and irrevocable differences. The middle class could not be aristocratic and the working class could hardly become bourgeois.

The conviction that there are real differences between social groups has practically disappeared in the course of the 20th century. Democracy and prosperity have produced a greater amount of social mobility and made the transitions from one social group to the next more fluid. However, in many cases former class distinctions are still observed nonetheless. An old and well-known aristocratic name carries some weight, and an academic is often treated with a higher degree of respect.

There are many different categories and subcategories of

Viennese and consequently many Viennese traditions. Manners and mannerisms, clothing, professions, and home addresses are rather accurate but not fool proof indicators of background. The value attached to each of these characteristics changes from milieu to milieu. What is acceptable in some circles is frowned upon in others.

The Viennese are bound to the earth in a peculiarly urban way. Moving out of their "home district" into a new one across town is a greater adjustment for many of them than for an American who moves from New York to Los Angeles. Many people regard the districts near *Grinzing* and *Schönbrunn* to be the best places to live in Vienna. However, excluding the upstarts, there are a great number of Viennese who would never move there even though they could afford to do so. By moving into a "noble" district, they would be denying their origins and could be accused of trying to be *etwas Besseres,* something better.

This physical sense of place or belonging is related to the way the Viennese view their rank in society. Social background is also reflected in the way the Viennese speak. There are many different categories of Viennese dialect. The refined upper class accent with is special intonation and vocabulary is frowned upon in working class circles just as the robust working class dialect is unacceptable in certain higher social circles. Simple linguistic traits like the pronunciation of the letter " *L*" speak volumes.

In addition to the various types of Viennese, there are different degrees of "Viennese-ness." If various social groups are distinguished and separated by their specific traditions, the Viennese are united by a common sense of tradition, of the way things have been and ought to be done. Some Viennese are — for better or for worse — more Viennese than others. The deterioration of traditional attitudes may be greeted by some as progress and lamented by others as decay. In any case, the conscious traditionalists and anti-traditionalists in Vienna are outnumbered by the habitual ones. Instead of consciously cultivating or fighting tradition, they live it.

Families at all social levels cultivate their heritage to a certain extent. More than elsewhere, lawyers' practices or pharmacies are passed from generation to generation. Professional groups cultivate social contacts which go beyond professional interests. Each one of them has an annual ball, and a physician, for example, might take his daughter to meet young colleagues in his field. A similar phenomena can be obeserved in butcher shops or bakeries where two to three generations work behind the counter. Scholarships at the University and other special programmes have been introduced to facilitate higher study for working class children, but they have not been as successful as planned. In spite of the incentives, the percentage of students with working class backgrounds is still disproportionately low. This is partially a consequence of a specific form of traditionalism.

The Viennese have a strong sense of precedent. Parents' expectations of their children are frequently related to the parameters of their own lives and social milieu. Money is no guarantee for an increase in social status. A new Mercedes and a big house will be recognized as achievements as long as their owners do not demonstratively try to jump up too many rungs on the social ladder. The Viennese sense of place and precedent makes social climbing an activity which is viewed with suspicion from above and below. Slipping down the social ladder is also an inexcusable transgression in many cases. The children of academics are frequently expected to be academics themselves. For example, failure to complete the university, not to mention the demanding secondary school of the *Gymnasium,* is a minor catastrophe. In some cases, a child's marriage to a person of unequal social background or the choice of a job outside of the family's long standing professional sphere may entail a loss of prestige.

It is difficult to trace certain traditional modes of behaviour and attitudes back to their origins. Peculiar to specific social groups, they may result in contradictory responses to the same things, but the results of different traditions may coincide, too. The Viennese virtues of modesty and measure may be Biedermeier in origin for certain middle class families that have conscientiously cultivated them for generations. On the other hand, they may be the consequences of post-World War I or II poverty in other families.

Traditionalism is also reflected in political behaviour. If someone tells you that he is an upper middle class practicing

Catholic, you can be relatively sure that he votes ÖVP. The same goes for the not religiously affiliated blue collar worker who votes SPÖ. The traditional conservative middle class families raise conservative children, and there are traditional socialist families, too. For many traditionalists, the younger generation of politicians are too smooth and self-aggrandizing, careerists and technocrats.

Leading members of the major parties youth organizations have become very popular by criticizing their parties own policies and authority structures, and environmentalists, *die Grünen* (Greens), are attracting supporters who are disillusioned with the policies and politics of the major parties. In December, 1984, an attempt to start construction on a large hydro-electric dam on the Danube near Hainburg east of Vienna met the resistance of environmentalists. They occupied the construction site in a rare natural habitat of the Danube lowlands which had to be cleared for construction to begin. A wave of popular sympathy — and unresolved legal questions — forced a stop to the work. The events surrounding Hainburg seem to indicate a shift in political attitudes, the consequences of which remain to be seen.

Nevertheless, the political parties benefit from traditional allegiances. For example, socialist parties throughout Europe have had trouble maintaining the second and the third generation offspring of their old supporters. Prosperity has drawn these children of socialists into other political circles. In Vienna, however, the socialist party has enjoyed a great deal of stability. Although many children of the older generation of socialists have made it, they have continued to vote socialist nevertheless. Many of these young socialists are not socialists by conviction like their parents but socialists by background or tradition.

These examples show how traditionalism is reflected in politics, but they are not intended to minimize the differences between Vienna's "old" and "new" or conservative and progressive political traditions. The SPÖ is very aware of its role and accomplishments as a working class party. The radicalism of the interwar period has disappeared, and since World War II the socialists have become the main proponents and the managers of the welfare state.

The socialists have their own heritage, a political subcul-
ture, which goes back to Red Vienna. Addressing fellow party
members as *Genosse* (comrade) is fundamentally a lip service
to party tradition, but some socialists still do not use the cus-
tomary Viennese greeting of *Grüß Gott* (God greet you)
because of its religious and clerical connotations. A stereotypi-
cal socialist may live in a *Gemeindebau* in a working class district, be the great-grandson of a 19th century Czech immigrant,
and after dying will be cremated instead of being buried at a
typically Viennese funeral.

The traditionalism of socialists and conservatives alike still
occasionally poisons the political atmosphere of the city. When
issues of principal difference cannot be resolved, the old interwar spirit of confrontation erupts again and each party drags
the other's political skeletons out of the closet to point out the
shortcomings of the opponent's predecessors and ideological
ancestors.

The socialists have expanded their social welfare programmes of the interwar period and successfully grafted the
welfare state onto Vienna's imperial cultural heritage. The
University of Pennsylvania recently published a global study on
the quality of life. Austria ranked fourth in the world behind the
Scandinavian trio of Sweden, Denmark, and Norway and far
ahead of other Western European and North American countries with higher standards of living. Criteria like the accessibility of culture, education, social security, crime rates, and medical services were used to quantify the concept of quality. Austria's high rating can be seen as the cumulative result of apparently divergent cultures. A tradition of social welfare has been
successfully integrated into Vienna's older cultural heritage.

Viennese traditionalism and Vienna's socialist tradition are
both being challenged — and to a certain extent undermined —
by that amorphous flood of commodities called mass or popular culture. This questionable form of cosmopolitan culture
came to Vienna later than elsewhere in Europe. The American
GIs with bubble gum and nylons may have been harbingers of
consumerism, but the four power occupation of Vienna actually retarded the city's post-war economic recovery. As a result,
the onset of prosperity, the necessary breeding ground for popular culture, was postponed. Vienna still lags behind the latest

trends to a certain extent, and some people have a simple and cynical rule-of-thumb: Vienna is always years behind.

Whether this lag in modernization is a matter of economic preconditions or Viennese dispositions is hard to determine, but there are certain advantages involved. Innovation is tested elsewhere before being adopted in Vienna. The allegedly out-dated often comes back into fashion after a few decades of modernization. Vienna's streetcars are a perfect example of this phenomenon. After World War II, many cities abandoned the "old fashioned" electric tram for the "modern" bus, but streetcars are now being re-introduced as an inexpensive and low pollution form of public transport.

Austria's economy is directed towards the international market, and this has brought an increasingly greater flood of commodities and innovations into the country. Prosperity has changed Vienna and the Viennese considerably. This is, of course, a modern phenomenon, but its effects are often more evident in Vienna because the city's sense of tradition is stronger than elsewhere. The viability and adaptability of Vienna's older cultural and political traditions is being tested by the specifically modern form of international culture which has been created by multinationals and mass communication.

☆ ☆ ☆

This book has attempted to refute the cliché as well as the coun-ter-cliché and show how Vienna's historical experiences have shaped the city. It remains to be seen what kind of Vienna past and present cultural forces will produce in the future.

Appendix

Time Line

8	The area around Vienna becomes part of the Roman province of *Pannonia*
98	Construction of the Roman *Limes,* a chain of fortifications along the Danube; permanent army camp of *Vindobona* established
180	The Roman emperor Marcus Aurelius dies (allegedly) in *Vindobona*
400	*Vindobona* mentioned for the last time in the official list of cities in the late Roman empire
433–453	Vienna area under the rule of the Huns
550	*Vindomina* mentioned in Jordanes' *History of the Goths*
570	Avars in the Vienna area
791–796	Charlemagne regains the territory around Vienna and allegedly passes Vienna
881	Salzburg annals mention a battle with the Hungarians *ad Weniam*
955	The German king Otto I defeats the Hungarians in the Battle of Lechfeld
976	First mention of the Babenbergs as margraves
996	First mention of the name *Ostarrichi* (Austria)
1114	Leopold III *der Heilige* (the Saint), canonized 1485, founds the abbey of *Klosterneuburg*
1137	Vienna mentioned as a *civitas* (city) in a contract between the Babenbergs and the diocese of Passau
1147	The bishop of Passau consecrates the "Vienna Church" of St. Stephen's
1155	Heinrich II *Jasomirgott* founds the *Schotten*-Abbey
1156	Austria gains the status of a hereditary duchy; Vienna becomes a ducal residence
1180–1198	Expansion of Vienna beyond the old Roman borders
1192	Richard the Lionharted prisoner of the Babenberg Leopold V

1214	Foundation of the University of Oxford
1221	First known municipal law of Vienna containing the staple law
1246	Friedrich II *der Streitbare* (the Quarrelsome) killed in a battle against the Hungarians; end of Babenberg dynasty and rule in Austria
1251–1276	Ottokar, King of Bohemia, rules in Vienna
1263	Second Romanesque church of St. Stephen's consecrated
1276	Rudolf von Habsburg besieges and occupies Vienna
1278	Ottokar killed in the Battle of Marchfeld; beginning of 640 years of Habsburg rule
1282	Rudolf invests his sons with the former Babenberg lands
1348	Emperor Karl IV establishes the first Central European university in Prague
1359	Rudolf IV begins Gothic expansion of St. Stephen's and orders building of south tower (nave is completed around 1450, tower in 1433)
1365	Rudolf IV founds the University of Vienna
1453	Turks conquer Constantinople
1455	Gutenberg invents movable metal print revolutionizing the production of books; first edition of Gutenberg's Bible
1462	The Viennese besiege Friedrich III in his castle
1469	Vienna becomes a bishopric
1485–1490	Vienna under Hungarian rule; Matthias Corvinus has his residence in the city
1492	Columbus discovers America
1496	Spanish marriage of Maximilian I's son establishes inheritance of Spanish realms
1498	Court Music Chapel founded by Maximilian I
1499	Switzerland gains independence from the Holy Roman Empire
1515	Double Marriage of Maximilian I's grandchildren establishes inheritance of Bohemia and Hungary
1517	Luther posts his 95 theses in Wittenberg
1521	The House of Habsburg separated into an Austrian and a Spanish line
1526	*De iure* acquisition of Bohemia and Moravia
1526	Ferdinand I ends autonomy of city government
1529	First Turkish siege of Vienna
1531–1566	Ring of Renaissance fortifications replaces medieval wall

1534	Ignatius of Loyola founds the Jesuit order in Paris
1543	Copernicus' theory of a heliocentric solar system
1545—1563	Council of Trent reforms Catholic Church and rejects concessions to Protestants
1551	Invited by Ferdinand I, Jesuits come to Vienna
1564	Death of Michelangelo; birth of Shakespeare
1566	First official registration of houses in Vienna; according to the register, 1,205 houses
1577	Protestant worship forbidden in Vienna
1584	*Il Gesú,* prototype of Baroque Jesuit church architecture, completed in Rome
1588	Spanish Armada defeated by the English
1603	"Monastery offensive" begins in Vienna
1604	Pilgrims land at Plymouth Rock
1618—1648	Thirty Years War
1625	Jesuits assume administration of University of Vienna
1625	First production of opera at the court in Vienna
1633	First Habsburg buried in the *Kapuzinergruft* (Imperial Burial Vault)
1636	Foundation of Harvard University
1645	Swedish troops threaten Vienna
1649	Charles I of England beheaded; Cromwell establishes the Commonwealth
1661—1710	Palace of Versailles built
1667	Production of the opera *Il Pomo d'Oro* in Vienna
1679	Plague ravages the population
1683	Second Turkish siege of Vienna
1687	Newton's *Philosophiae naturalis principia mathematica*
1695	Work started on *Schönbrunn* palace (first plan)
1697—1717	Prince Eugen's campaigns against the Turks
1704	*Linienwall* (second ring of fortifications) constructed to protect the suburbs
1701—1714	War of Spanish Succession
1713	Plague in Vienna
1714—1723	Construction of Lower and Upper *Belvedere*
1716—1737	Work on *Karlskirche*
1723—1726	Construction of *Hofbibliothek* (Court Library)
1744	Porcelain manufacture established in the *Augarten*
1744—1779	Reconstruction of *Schönbrunn;* Pacassi commissioned by Maria Theresia
1766	Joseph II opens *Prater* to the public
1769	Watt invents steam engine

1771	Houses in Vienna numbered
1776	American Declaration of Independence; abolition of torture in Austria
1781	Joseph's II Patent of Tolerance; Mozart settles in Vienna
1782	Suspension of monasteries begins; Pope Pius VI visits Vienna
1784	*Allgemeines Krankenhaus* (General Hospital) opened
1789	French Revolution begins
1791	Mozart's *Magic Flute* performed in Vienna
1792	Beethoven settles in Vienna
1793	Louis XVI and Marie Antoinette executed in Paris; first production of Haydn's *Creation*
1804	Franz I Emperor of Austria
1805	Napoleon occupies Vienna
1806	End of the Holy Roman Empire
1809	Second Napoleonic occupation of Vienna; Austrian victory at Aspern and defeat at Wagram near Vienna
1811	National bankruptcy declared in Austria
1812	Foundation of *Gesellschaft der Musikfreunde*
1814—15	Congress of Vienna
1815	Establishment of the *Technische Hochschule* (Technical College) in Vienna
1816	First Christmas tree in Vienna
1822	Schubert's *Unfinished Symphony*
1830	Flood of the Danube
1831—32	Cholera epidemic in Vienna
1833	Abolition of slavery in England
1837	First steam driven locomotive starts operating east of Vienna (Floridsdorf — Deutsch Wagram)
1837—1901	Reign of Queen Victoria of England
1842	First Philharmonic Concert organized in Vienna
1845	First gas installations in Vienna
1848	Revolutionary uprisings in Paris, Milan, Venice, Cracow, Prague, Pest; revolution in Vienna (March—October)
1848—1916	Reign of Emperor Franz Joseph I
1848—1854	*Semmering* railway constructed
1850	Suburbs incorporated into city of Vienna; 9 districts, population of 431,000
1851	First World Exhibition in London
1852	H. Beecher-Stowe's *Uncle Tom's Cabin*

1861	Beginning of the liberal era of city administration (until 1895)
1861–1865	American Civil War
1862	Flood of the Danube; Brahms settles in Vienna
1865	First horse drawn tramways; first section of *Ringstraße* opened
1867	Suez Canal opened; *Ausgleich* (Compromise) with Hungary; Austro-Hungarian Empire established; Austrian constitution guarantees fundamental rights
1869	Opera House on the *Ringstraße* opened
1872	Franz Grillparzer dies in Vienna
1872–1874	Construction begins on the Museums, the *Rathaus,* Parliament, University, Stock-Exchange and *Burgtheater*
1873	First aqueduct opened
1873	First World Exhibition in Vienna; crash of stock exchange
1874	10th district *(Favoriten)* established; opening of *Zentralfriedhof* (Central Cemetry); premiere of Johann Strauß' *Fledermaus*
1875	Regulation of the Danube completed
1879	*Votivkirche* opened; great parade on the *Ringstraße* celebrating the silver wedding anniversary of the imperial couple *(Makart-Festzug)*
1881	Construction of *Neue Hofburg* (new wing of imperial residence) begins
1888–89	Social Democratic Party unified
1889	Crown Prince Rudolf commits suicide in Mayerling
1890	First May Day parade of Viennese workers
1893	*Christlich-Soziale Partei* (Christian-Social Party) founded (formerly the *Christlich-sozialer Verein,* 1887)
1890–1892	*Linienwall* razed; suburbs incorporated; 19 districts; population of 1,365,000
1895–1902	*Stadtbahn* transit system constructed
1896	Anton Bruckner dies in Vienna; Theodor Herzl's *Der Judenstaat* (The Jewish State) published
1897	Secession founded, construction of the *Secession* building started
1897–1907	Gustav Mahler director of Vienna Opera
1897–1910	Dr. Karl Lueger mayor of Vienna
1899	Sigmund Freud's *Interpretation of Dreams* published

1903	*Wiener Werkstätte* (Vienna Workshop) founded
1904—1906	Postal Savings Bank built by Otto Wagner
1905	*Die lustige Witwe* (The Merry Widow) by Franz Lehar; world premiere in Vienna
1905	Bertha von Suttner wins Nobel Peace Prize
1907	Universal male suffrage introduced
1910	Second aqueduct finished
1911	*Rosenkavalier* (music by Richard Strauss, libretto by Hugo von Hofmannsthal) produced in Vienna
1914—1918	World War I
1916	Death of Emperor Franz Joseph
1918	Karl I renounces responsibility for goverment; the Republic of German-Austria proclaimed
1919	Peace Treaty with Austria signed in St. Germain; socialists win municipal elections in Vienna
1920	Austria becomes a federal state; constitution adopted
1922	Mussolini comes to power in Italy (fascist rule); Vienna becomes a province; separation from Lower Austria
1923	Vienna starts communal building programme
1927	*Schattendorf* trial; Palace of Justice in Vienna set on fire
1929	The Great Depression begins
1930	*Karl Marx Hof* completed
1933	Hitler comes to power in Germany (January); Dollfuß ends parliamentary democracy in Austria (March)
1934	Civil war between conservatives and socialists in Austria (February); Dollfuß killed during Nazi putsch attempt (July)
1938	*Anschluß,* Hitler's troops occupy Austria
1939—1945	World War II
1943	Battle of Stalingrad ends; Moscow Declaration issued by Allies (November)
1944—45	Heavy bombing of Vienna (52 air raids)
1945	Soviet troops take Vienna; Second Republic proclaimed; first concert and theatre performances (April); occupation of Austria, Four Power control begins in Vienna (September); first democratic elections since 1930 (November)
1945—1966	ÖVP-SPÖ coalition governments
1947	Negotiation of State Treaty starts

1948	Austria begins to receive Marshall Plan aid; communists take power in Hungary and Czechoslovakia
1950—1953	Korean War
1952	Choir of St. Stephen's re-opened, *Pummerin* (bell) recast
1953	Stalin's death
1955	Austrian State Treaty signed and ratified; end of Allied occupation, Austria proclaims permanent neutrality; Opera and *Burgtheater* re-opened after reconstruction
1956	Hungarian Revolution; 200,000 Hungarian refugees in Austria
1957	International Atomic Energy Agency moves to Vienna
1961	Kennedy and Khrushchev meet in Vienna; Berlin Wall erected
1967	United Nations Industrial Development Organization moves permanent seat to Vienna
1970	Bruno Kreisky forms socialist government (remains federal chancellor until 1983)
1970	SALT conference in Vienna
1971	SALT talks in Vienna
1978	*U-Bahn* (first phase) completed
1979	Carter and Breshnev meet in Vienna
1979	UNO City (Vienna International Centre) opened
1984	Danube Island completed; second phase of *U-Bahn* begun

In Vienna

The following suggestions are "illustrations" for the individual chapters. More detailed information is available in guide books or literature normally to be found at the individual sites. The Historical Museum of the City of Vienna, 1040, Karlsplatz 8, has an excellent permanent exhibition which covers the development of the city from prehistoric times to the present.

I. Foundations

Roman Ruins: 1010, Hoher Markt 3
Borders of Roman Encampment: 1010, Naglergasse—Graben—Kramergasse—Rotgasse—Salzgries—Tiefer Graben

Ecclesiastical buildings:
St. Ruprecht's: 1010, Ruprechtsplatz
St. Stephen's: 1010, Stephansplatz (Western facade)
St. Michael's: 1010, Michaelerplatz (walls seen from the courtyard of
    Michaelerplatz 6 and from the courtyard of Kohlmarkt 11)
Schottenstift (*Finstere Sakristei*, relics of original Romanesque basi-
    lica): 1010, Freyung 6
Virgilkapelle: 1010, Stephansplatz (U Bahn-station)

II. Conflicts and Consolidation

Ecclesiastical buildings:
Augustinerkirche: 1010, Augustinerstraße
Maria am Gestade: 1010, Salvatorgasse
Minoritenkirche: 1010, Minoritenplatz
Salvatorkapelle: 1010, Salvatorgasse 5 (entrance)
Schottenstift: 1010, Freyung 6 (winged altar-piece of the Schotten-
    meister)
St. Stephan's: 1010, Stephansplatz

Secular buildings:
Amalientrakt: 1010, Hofburg
Renaissance Courtyard: 1010, Bäckerstraße 7
Schweizer Tor: 1010, Hofburg
Stallburg: 1010, Reitschulgasse 2

Parish churches in the suburbs:
1130, Hietzinger Platz
1190, Himmelstraße 25
1190, Fröschelgasse 20

III. Baroque: A Festive Society and Onlooking Masses

Ecclesiastical buildings:
Jesuitenkirche: 1010, Dr. Ignaz Seipel-Platz
Karlskirche: 1040, Karlsplatz
Peterskirche: 1010, Petersplatz
Piaristenkirche (Maria Treu): 1080, Jodok Fink-Platz
Salesianerinnenkirche: 1030, Rennweg 10

Secular buildings:
Auersperg Palace: 1080, Auerspergstraße 1
Belvedere Palaces: 1040, Prinz-Eugen-Straße 27
Böhmische Hofkanzlei: 1010, Wipplingerstraße 7 and Judenplatz 11
    (Verfassungsgerichtshof, Verwaltungsgerichtshof)

Bürgerliches Zeughaus: 1010, Am Hof 10 (former armory, now fire department)
Finanzministerium: 1010, Himmelpfortgasse 4—8 (former Winter Palace of Prince Eugene)
Liechtenstein Palace: 1090, Fürstengasse 1 (now Museum of Modern Art)
Österreichische Nationalbibliothek: 1010, Josephsplatz
Schönbrunn: 1130, Schönbrunner Schloßstraße 13
Schwarzenberg Palace: 1030, Rennweg 2
Trautson Palace: 1070, Museumstraße 7
Other Palaces: 1010, around Freyung, Herrengasse, Bankgasse, Minoritenplatz, Lobkowitzplatz

Fountains:
1010, Neuer Markt
1010, Wipplingerstraße 8 (courtyard of Altes Rathaus)
1010, Hoher Markt

Monuments:
Mariensäule: 1010, Am Hof
Pestsäule: 1010, Graben

IV. Enlightenment: An Attempt at Welfare

Akademie der Wissenschaften: 1010, Dr. Ignaz Seipel Platz 2 (old University building)
Albertina (Palais Taroucca): 1010, Augustinerstraße 1 (Print collection)
Allgemeines Krankenhaus: 1090, Alserstraße 4 (General Hospital)
Gardekirche: 1030, Rennweg 5a
Josephinum: 1090, Währingerstraße 25 (Institute of the History of Medicine)
Kaisergruft: 1010, Neuer Markt (Imperial Burial Vault)
Lusthaus: 1020, Prater Hauptallee
Schubladkastenhaus: 1010, Freyung 7

V. Biedermeier: A Culture of the Home

Äußeres Burgtor: 1010, Burgring
Bundesmobiliensammlung: 1070, Mariahilferstraße 88 (Federal Collection of Period Furniture)
Clam-Gallas palace: 1090, Währingerstraße 30 (Lycée Francais de Vienne)
Geymüllerschlössel: 1180, Khevenhüllerstraße 2 (Clock collection)

Pötzleinsdorfer Schloß: 1180, Geymüllergasse 1
Schottenhof: 1010, Freyung 6
St. Marxer Friedhof: 1030, Leberstraße (Biedermeier cemetary)
Synagogue: 1010, Seitenstettengasse 2—4
Technische Universität: 1040, Karlsplatz 13

VI. The New Dimensions of the Ringstraße

Buildings on the Ringstraße:
Börse: 1010, Schottenring 16 (Stock Exchange)
Burgtheater: 1010, Dr.-Karl-Lueger-Ring
Kunsthistorisches Museum: 1010, Burgring
Naturhistorisches Museum: 1010, Burgring
Museum für Angewandte Kunst: 1010, Stubenring (Applied Arts)
Neue Hofburg: 1010, Burgring
Oper: 1010, Opernring
Parlament: 1010, Dr.-Karl-Renner-Ring
Rathaus: 1010, Rathausplatz
Regierungsgebäude: 1010, Stubenring (former Ministry of Defence)
Roßauer Kaserne: 1090, Schlickplatz
Universität: 1010, Dr.-Karl-Lueger-Ring

Some former privately owned Ringstraße-buildings:
Hotel Imperial: 1010, Kärntner Ring (Württemberg Palace)
OPEC Centre: 1010, Dr.-Karl-Lueger-Ring (Deutschmeisterpa-
    lais)
Wiener Stadtschulrat: 1010, Dr.-Karl-Renner-Ring (Epstein
    Palace)

Other important buildings built during the period:
Equitable Palace: 1010, Stock im Eisen-Platz 4
Handelsakademie: 1010, Akademiestraße 12
Hermesvilla: 1130, Lainzer Tiergarten
Justizpalast: 1010, Schmerlingplatz 10
Künstlerhaus: 1010, Karlsplatz 5
Musikverein: 1010, Dumbastraße 3

Ecclesiastical buildings:
Votivkirche: 1090, Rooseveltplatz
Maria vom Siege: 1150, Mariahilfer Gürtel
St. Francis': 1020, Mexikoplatz

Interior:
Kaiserapartments: 1010, Hofburg (Imperial Apartments)

VII. Breaking with the Past: Modern Sensibilities

Secession: 1010, Friedrichstraße 12
Freud-Museum: 1090, Berggasse 19

Villas by Joseph Hoffmann:
1030, Gloriettegasse 14—16
1190, Nußwaldgasse 20
1190, Steinfeldgasse 2
1190, Steinfeldgasse 4
1190, Wollergasse 10
1190, Wollergasse 12

Buildings by Adolf Loos:
1010, Michaelerplatz 3
1130, Larochegasse 3
1180, Starkfriedgasse 19

Café Museum: 1010, Friedrichstraße 6
Kärntner Bar: 1010, Kärntner Durchgang
Knize: 1010, Graben (Clothing Store)

Buildings by Otto Wagner:
1060, Linke Wienzeile 38
1060, Linke Wienzeile 40
1070, Döblergasse 2
1070, Döblergasse 4
1070, Neustiftgasse 40
1140, Hüttelbergstraße 26 (villa)
1140, Hüttelbergstraße 28 (villa)

Kirche am Steinhof: 1140, Baumgartner Höhe 1
Österreichische Postsparkasse: 1010 Georg-Coch-Platz 2 (Austrian
    Postal Savings Bank)
Stadtbahn-Stations (e.g. 1010, Karlsplatz)

VIII. The Imperial Capital Becomes a Socialist Stronghold

1030, Museum of Military History, Arsenal, Objekt 18

Gemeindebauten (selection):
Reumanhof: 1050, Margareten Gürtel 100—110
George Washington Hof: 1120, Unter Meidlingerstraße 1—12
Sandleiten: 1160, Matteotti-Platz
Karl Marx Hof: 1190, in between Heiligenstädterstraße and Bosch-
    straße
Engelshof: 1200, Engelsplatz

IX. The Nazi Interlude: Vienna, Germany

Documentation Archive of the Austrian Resistance (exhibition):
Wipplingerstraße 8, Stiege 3
Anti-aircraft towers:
1020, Augarten Park
1030, Arenberg Park
1060, Esterhazy Park
1070, Mariahilferkaserne, Stiftsgasse

X. The Aftermath: Allied Occupation

Monument to the Red Army: 1030, Schwarzenbergplatz

XI. Old Problems and New Impulses

Vienna International Centre: 1220, Wagramer Straße
Wien 2000, (exhibition): 1060, Messepalast

Suggested Readings in English

Richard Rickett's *A Brief Survey of Austrian History* (Prachner: Vienna, 1966, 7th ed., 1983) is, in spite of some minor flaws, still the best short introduction to Austrian history. For the musically interested, Rickett has also written *Music and Musicians in Vienna* (Prachner: Vienna, 1973). Günther Feuerstein's *Vienna: Past and Present* (Jugend und Volk: Vienna, 1974, 2nd ed., 1979) consists of three short, well illustrated volumes. These books are good introductory texts. David Pryce-Jones' *Vienna* from the Time-Life series "Great Cities" (Time-Life International: Amsterdam, 1978), also includes an insightful photo essay by Thomas Höpker. William Johnston's *The Austrian Mind: An Intellectual and Social History 1848–1938* (University of California Press: Berkely, 1972; paperback, 1983) is a sophisticated and ambitious analysis which also may be used as a reference work. A tremendous number of books dealing with Vienna around the turn of the century have recently been published, therefore only a representative sample will be mentioned here. Frederic Morton's *Nervous Splendor: Vienna 1888–1889* (Little, Brown, and Co.: Boston, 1979) is a well written narrative of events leading up to the suicide of Crown Prince Rudolph in 1889 which vividly captures the spirit of the times. J. Sydney Jones' *Hitler in Vienna: 1907–1913* (Stem and Day: New York, 1983) is an

194

equally accessible work which portrays the atmosphere and personalities of late imperial Vienna as well as the influence the city exercised on Hitler during his formative years. Carl E. Schorske's prize winning collection of essays, *Fin de Siècle Vienna: Politics and Culture,* (Knopf: New York, 1980; Vintage paperback, 1981) is a provocative and scholarly analysis of Vienna at the turn of the century. *Wittgenstein's Vienna* by Allan Janik and Stephen Toulmin (Simon and Schuster: 1971; 2nd ed. Torchbook paperback, 1983) interprets Wittgenstein in light of his Viennese background and is recommended for the philosophically inclined reader. Christian Nebehay's *Vienna 1900: Architecture and Painting* (Verlag Christian Brandstätter: Vienna, 1984) is a valuable book which also includes a guide that enables readers to track down individual buildings or paintings in Vienna. Similar works by Nebehay dealing with music and literature are scheduled to appear in the near future. Edward Chrankshaw, author of a number of books on the history of the Habsburg empire, also has written an interwar retrospect, *Vienna: The Image of a Culture in Decline* (MacMillan: London, 1938; reprint, 1978). A historical and an autobiographical work by George Clare, *Last Waltz in Vienna: The Destruction of a Jewish Family 1842−1942* (MacMillan: London, 1981; Pan Paperback, 1982), provides a lucid narrative of important historical events while tracing four generations of his family's history from assimilation to Auschwitz. Last but not least, Graham Greene's novel, *The Third Man,* vividly captures the atmosphere of post-World War II Vienna under Allied occupation.

Selected Bibliography

Andics, Hellmut, *Der Staat, den keiner wollte* and *Die Insel der Seligen* (Molden: Vienna, 1968; 2nd revised edition, Goldmann, 1984)

Botz, Gerhard, *Wien vom Anschluß zum Krieg* (Jugend und Volk: Vienna, 1978)

Csendes, Peter, *Geschichte Wiens* (Verlag für Geschichte und Politik: Vienna, 1981)

Czeike, Felix, *Geschichte der Stadt Wien* (Molden: Vienna, 1981)

Czeike, Felix (ed.), *Wien: 1938* (Verein für Geschichte der Stadt Wien: Vienna, 1978)

Czeike, Felix (ed.), *Das große Groner Wien-Lexikon* (Molden: Vienna, 1977)

Ehalt, Hubert, *Ausdrucksformen Absolutistischer Herrschaft* (Verlag f. Geschichte u. Politik: Vienna, 1980)

Elias, Norbert, *Die höfische Gesellschaft* (Soziologische Texte 54, 1969)

Heindl, Gottfried, *Und die Größe ist gefährlich* (Neff: Vienna/Berlin, 1969)

Hennings, Fred, *Das barocke Wien,* (Herold: Vienna/Munich, 1965)

Hennings, Fred, *Das josephinische Wien* (Herold: Vienna/Munich, 1966)

Hennings, Fred, *Ringstraßensymphonie* (Herold: Vienna/Munich, 1963)

Kann, Robert A., *A History of the Habsburg Empire 1526—1918* (University of California Press: Berkely, second ed., 1977)

Kleindel, Walter, *Österreich: Daten zur Geschichte und Kultur* (Ueberreuter: Vienna, 1978)

Luza, Radomir, *Austro-German Relations in the Anschluss Era* (Princeton University Press: New Jersey, 1975)

. Magistrat der Stadt Wien, Geschäftsgruppe Stadtplanung, *Statistisches Taschenbuch der Stadt Wien* (Vorwärts: Vienna, 1983)

Perfahl, Josef, ed., *Wien Chronik* (Bergland Buch: Salzburg/Stuttgart, 1961)

Schmidt, Erwin, *Wiener Stadtgeschichte* (Jugend und Volk: Vienna, 3rd revised ed., 1978)

Schulmeister, Otto (ed.), *Spectrum Austriae* (Molden: Vienna/Munich/Zurich, 2nd ed., 1977)

Schüssel, Therese, and Zöllner, Erich, *Das Werden Österreichs* (Österreichischer Bundesverlag u. Verlag f. Geschichte und Politik: Vienna, 1964)

Sotriffer, Kristian (ed.), *Das größere Österreich* (Edition Tusch: Vienna, 1982)

Stadler, Karl, *Austria* (Benn: London, 1971)

Stadler, Karl, *Österreich 1938—1945 im Spiegel der NS-Akten* (Herold: Vienna, 1966)

Steinbach, J., and Feilmayer, W., *Analysen der Wiener Stadtstruktur* (Magistrat der Stadt Wien: Vienna, 1983)

Steiner, Kurt (ed.), *Tradition and Innovation in Modern Austria* (SPOSS: Palo Alto, 1982)

Sully, Melanie, *Continuity and Change in Austrian Socialism* (Columbia University Press: New York, 1982)

Vergo, Peter, *Art in Vienna: 1898—1918* (Phaidon: London, 1975)

Waissenberger, Robert (ed.), *Wien 1870–1930: Traum und Wirklichkeit* (Residenz Verlag: Salzburg, 1984)
Weinzierl, Erika, and Skalnik, Kurt (ed.), *Österreich: die Erste Republik* (Styria: Graz/Vienna/Cologne, 1983)
Weinzierl, Erika, and Skalnik, Kurt (ed.), *Österreich: die Zweite Republik* (Styria: Graz/Vienna/Cologne, 1972)
Ziak, Karl (ed.), *Unvergängliches Wien* (Europa Verlag: Vienna 1964)

Index

Abraham a Sancta Clara   41
Adler, Alfred   117
Adler, Victor   94, 96
Alt, Rudolph von   83
Altenburg, Peter   113
Amerling, Friedrich von   83

Badoni, Pompeo   62
Bahr, Hermann   113
Báráni, Robert   116
Bauer Otto   125
Ben Gurion, David   115
Beethoven, Ludwig van   82, 155, 166, 186
Berg, Alban   127
Billroth, Theodor   116
Böhm-Bawerk, Eugen von   117
Bonfini, Antonio de   36
Borromeo, Carlo   43
Brahms, Johannes   82, 109, 149, 187
Breshnev, Leonid   173, 189
Bruckner, Anton   82, 109 f., 187
Bürckel, Josef   142, 144

Canaletto   51
Canevale, Isidore   64
Carter, Jimmy   173, 189
Celtes, Konrad   30
Charlemagne   183
Codefroy, Jean   77
Corvinus, Matthias   29, 36, 184
Cuspinian, Johannes   30

Daffinger, Moritz Michael   83
Danhauser, Joseph   83
Daun, Leopold Joseph, Graf   60
Doderer, Heimito von   11
Dollfuß, Engelbert   134 f., 137, 188

Eichmann, Adolf   144
Eleonora, Empress   53
Elisabeth, Empress   103
Esterhazy-family   71
Eugen, Prinz von Savoyen   44 f., 51, 58, 101, 185

Fendi, Peter   83
Ferdinand I, Holy Roman Emperor   31, 37 f., 184 f.
Ferdinand I, Emperor of Austria   77, 87
Ferdinand III   53
Ferstel, Heinrich von   103
Figl, Leopold   165
Fischer von Erlach, Johann Bernhard   43, 46 ff.,
Fischer von Erlach, Joseph Emanuel   47
Franz Ferdinand, Archduke   119
Franz Joseph I   87, 89, 91, 93, 96, 103 f., 110, 119, 186, 188
Franz Stephan von Lothringen, Holy Roman Emperor   60, 72
Freud, Sigmund   111 f., 116 f., 127, 141, 187

Friedrich II der Streitbare 22, 184
Friedrich II, King of Prussia 58, 61
Friedrich III, Holy Roman Emperor 27 ff., 184
Fuchs, Maria Karolina, Countess 60

Gluck, Christoph Willibald 50, 71, 82
Grillparzer, Franz 85, 155, 187

Hansen, Theophil von 100, 103
Hanslick, Eduard 109
Hasenauer, Karl von 101
Hauer, Joseph Matthias 127
Haydn, Joseph 50, 71, 82
Hebra, Ferdinand von 116
Heinrich II, Jasomirgott 17, 21, 183
Herzl, Theodor 115, 187
Heuberger, Richard 111
Hildebrandt, Lukas von 47
Hirschvogel, Augustin 33
Hitler, Adolf 97, 134, 137 ff., 146, 156, 188
Hoefnagel, Jakob 33
Hoffmann, Joseph 108
Hofmannsthal, Hugo von 113, 127, 188
Huber, Joseph Daniel 68−69
Hyrtl, Josef 116

Ignatius of Loyola 37, 185

Jefferson, Thomas 61
John Paul II 64
Jordanes 183
Joseph I 47
Joseph II 61 ff., 70 ff., 79, 185, 186

Karl I 119 ff., 188
Karl IV 25, 184
Karl V 31
Karl VI 43, 47, 52, 58
Karl, Archduke 75 f.
Karl von Lothringen 43 f.

Kaunitz, Prince Wenzel Anton 60
Kelsen, Hans 117
Kennedy, John F. 173, 189
Khlesl Melchior 39
Khrushchev, Nikita 173, 189
Klimt, Gustav 102
Koltschitzky, Georg Franz 44
Körner Theodor 154 f.
Kornhäusel, Joseph Georg 80
Kraus, Karl 114, 127
Krauss, Clemens 155
Kreisky, Bruno 173, 189

Lacius, Wolfgang 36
Lanner, Joseph 82
Leopold I, Holy Roman Emperor 43, 47, 53
Leopold II, Holy Roman Emperor, (Grand Duke of Tuscany) 60, 62, 74
Leopold III 22, 183
Leopold V 18, 183
Lueger, Karl 92 ff., 124, 144, 187
Ligne, Karl Joseph Prince de 76
Loos, Adolf 113 f., 127
Louis XIV 49
Luther, Martin 37, 184

Mahler, Gustav 82, 110, 113, 142, 187
Makart, Hans 103, 106
Marcus Aurelius 15, 183
Maria of Burgundy 29
Maria Louise 76
Maria Theresia 58 ff., 70 ff., 185
Marie Antoinette 74, 186
Maximilian I 29 ff., 184
Maximilian II 38
Menger, Karl 117
Merian, Matthäus 33, 35
Metternich, Clemens Wenzel Lothar, Prince 76 ff., 85, 87
Meytens, Martin van 59
Millöcker, Karl 111
Mises, Ludwig von 141
Montagu, Lady Mary 50
Moser, Kolo 108

198

Mozart, Wolfgang Amadeus   50,
   54, 71, 72 f., 82, 186
Musil, Robert   141
Mussolini, Benito   134, 188

Napoleon   75 f.
Nestroy, Johann   84
Nicholas II   115
Niclas Gerhaert van Leyden   28
Nüll, Eduard van der   100

Olbrich, Josef Maria   108
Otto I   15, 183
Ottokar, King of Bohemia   24,
   29, 184

Piccolomini, Aeneas Silvius   33
Pirquet, Clemens von   116
Pius VI   63, 186
Preminger, Otto   142
Prykril, Josef   154

Raimund, Ferdinand   84
Reed, Carol   162
Reinhardt, Max   113, 142
Renner, Karl   121 f., 154 f.
Richard the Lionhearted   18 f.,
   183
Rokitansky, Karl von   116
Roth, Joseph   127
Rudolf von Habsburg   24 ff., 184
Rudolf IV   25 ff., 184

Schärf, Adolf   174
Schirach, Baldur von   146
Schmidt, Friedrich von   101
Schmeltzl, Wolfgang   36
Schnitzler, Arthur   111 f.
Schöffel, Joseph   93
Schönberg, Arnold   127, 141
Schönerer, Georg von   97
Schrödinger, Erwin   141
Schubert, Franz   82 f., 155, 186
Schuschnigg, Kurt von   137 f.

Seitz, Karl   136
Semmelweis, Ignaz Philipp   116
Semper, Gottfried   101
Seyss-Inquart, Arthur   138
Sicardsburg, August Sicard
   von   100
Skoda, Joseph   116
Sobieski, Jan   43
Soliman II   32
Sonnenfels, Joseph von   60
Stalin, Joseph   165, 189
Starhemberg, Ernst Rüdiger Graf
   von   43
Stifter, Adalbert   85
Stoclet, Adolphe   109
Strauss, Richard   127, 188
Strauß, Johann (father)   82
Strauß, Johann (son)   110, 111,
   187
Suppé, Franz von   111
Suttner, Bertha von   114 f.
Swieten, Gerhard van   60

Tandler, Julius   128
Tschaikowskij, Peter Iljitsch   155
Torberg, Friedrich   141

Wärndorfer, Fritz   108
Wagner, Otto   105 f., 108, 131
Wagner, Richard   110, 113, 149
Wagner-Jauregg, Julius von   116
Waldmüller, Ferdinand
   Georg   83
Walther von der Vogelweide   17
Walter, Bruno   141
Welles, Orson   162
Webern, Anton von   127
Weigel, Hans   11, 81
Werfel, Franz   141
Wilder, Thornton   84
Wieser, Friedrich von   117
Wilson, Woodrow   119
Wittgenstein, Ludwig   127

Zweig, Stefan   141

Picture Credits